SMALL WORLD CELEBRATIONS

By Jean Warren and Elizabeth McKinnon
Illustrated by Marion Hopping Ekberg

Warren Publishing House, Inc.
Everett, Washington

Copy Editor: Brenda Mann Harrison
Production Manager: Gayle Bittinger
Production Assistant: Deborah Bori
Typesetting and Design: Mary Barrett, Image by Design
Layout: Kathy Jones and Cora Bunn
Cover Design: Kathy Jones

ISBN 0-911019-19-7

Library of Congress Catalog Number 88-050594
Printed in the United States of America
Published by: Warren Publishing House, Inc.
          P.O. Box 2250
          Everett, WA 98203

THE CHILDREN'S SONG

Listen to the children
Listen to their song
Voices filled with hope
Come and sing along.

Listen to their future
Listen to their theme
One world for all to share
Listen to their dream!

Listen to the rhythm
Peace across the land
Listen to the promise
Children hand-in-hand.

Come and raise your voices
Come and sing along
Fill the world with harmony
Sing the Children's Song!

Jean Warren, 1988

Contents

Introduction

Small World Celebrations is designed as a multicultural resource for teachers of young children.

In the book you will find fun, easy suggestions for using holidays and festivals to introduce your children to fifteen different cultures. Each chapter contains an introduction that explains how children from a particular culture celebrate a major holiday or festival, plus suggestions for art, learning games, language, science, movement, music and snacks. The activities offer ample opportunities for your children to experience aspects of both the celebration and the culture through seeing, hearing, touching, smelling and tasting. Each activity has been carefully chosen for its appropriateness as well as for its simplicity. And each uses materials that are readily available. By building on the familiar as each culture is introduced, your children can come to appreciate similarities as well as differences.

Following the activities in each chapter, you will find a folktale from the particular culture that has been especially adapted for young listeners. Folktales are universal, making them natural bridges between cultures. Because your children can easily identify with the stories, they will come to learn that children all over the world share similar fantasies, hopes and dreams.

Although *Small World Celebrations* is primarily designed to provide young children with an introduction to cultural appreciation, many of the activities also can be used with older children as part of more comprehensive teaching units. To enrich your celebrations, you may wish to consider the following suggestions:

- Set out library books about different cultures that contain pictures of children, families, homes, holiday celebrations, etc.
- Play library recording of ethnic songs and music.
- Display items from different cultures such as toys, eating utensils, art and craft objects and articles of clothing.
- Invite parents or older students from different cultures to come in and teach songs or games or help prepare authentic snacks.
- Plan field trips to such places as museums, ethnic centers, international food and import shops and ethnic restaurants.
- Check travel agencies or major airline offices for travel posters to use as room decorations. Check also for illustrated travel brochures that can be cut up and used to make matching picture games.

Note: Some of the celebrations in this book take place on different dates each year. To find out the exact date of a holiday or a festival, check your local library.

7

Winter Festival

A Russian Celebration

WINTER FESTIVAL
A Russian Celebration

For children in Russia, the Winter Festival at New Year's time is a very special holiday. It begins in late December when streets and shop windows come alive with twinkling lights, tinsel and frosty snowman decorations. The children and their families join holiday crowds to shop for New Year's presents and for fir trees to take home and decorate with gaily colored ornaments.

On New Year's Eve the children wait eagerly for a visit from Grandfather Frost and his helper, Snow Girl. Grandfather Frost looks like Santa Claus with his red robe, long white beard and black boots. Shaking his jingle bells, he gives presents to the children and wishes them all a Happy New Year.

Throughout the holiday the children attend many New Year's parties. The parties take place around decorated New Year's trees with music and other entertainment for the children to enjoy. Of course, Grandfather Frost and Snow Girl always make an appearance to hand out little decorated bags filled with fruits or sweets. The most elaborate party is held in a public hall in Moscow around a giant New Year's tree. Thousands of children take part in the festivities that include folk dancers, singers, clowns, magicians and actors dressed as animals and fairy tale characters.

Since the Winter Festival lasts until January 5, the children have plenty of time for outdoor activities. They spend many hours playing in the snow, ice skating or sledding in the large public parks. And, if they are very lucky, they can enjoy the traditional custom of riding in sleighs that are pulled across the snow by *troikas* (three-team horses).

SPARKLING SNOWMEN

Let the children make snowman decorations for your Winter Festival celebration. Give each child a large snowman shape cut from white construction paper. Whip Ivory Snow powder with water until the mixture is soft and fluffy. Have the children fingerpaint with the mixture on their snowman shapes. While the mixture is still wet, let them stick on black construction paper circles to make snowman faces. Then let them sprinkle on silver glitter or small pieces of tinsel to add sparkle. Allow the shapes to dry before mounting them on a wall or a bulletin board.

FUR HATS

Fur hats are very popular in Russia where the winters are long and cold. To make a hat for each child, cut off the bottom half of a white or brown paper sack (about 7 inches wide) and roll up the cut edges. Let the children tear cotton balls into thin wispy pieces. Then have them brush glue on their hats and place the cotton pieces on top of the glue for fur.

STORYTIME FUN

Read or tell the Russian folktale "Snow Girl" on p. 17. Talk with the children about why Snow Girl didn't like to play in the sunshine and why she had to leave when spring came. Then have them pretend to be frozen snow children who magically come to life as you name different body parts.

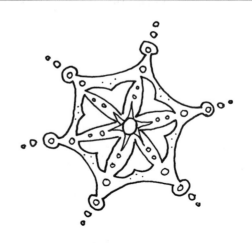

11

NESTING DOLLS

Among the favorite New Year's toys in Russia are "little mother" nesting dolls. The brightly painted dolls are made out of wood and fit one inside the other. If possible, bring in a set of these dolls. (Check international gift shops or import stores.) Or let the children make their own sets of nesting dolls using three different sizes of Styrofoam cups. Draw identical faces and bodies on the sides of the cups and have the children add details with felt-tip markers. Then let them have fun nesting their dolls one inside the other and lining them up from smallest to largest.

MELTING AND FREEZING

Place ice cubes in paper cups. Put one cup outside and let the children place the others in different parts of the room (close to a window, close to a heater, in a refrigerator, on a tabletop, etc.). Later, have the children check the cups and observe what happened to the ice. Did some cubes melt faster than others? Why? How could they make the cubes melt really fast? When all the ice has melted, pour the water into an ice cube tray and place it in the freezer. Remove the tray periodically to let the children observe as the water turns back into ice.

Variation: If there is snow in your area, use snowballs instead of ice cubes and ask the children to predict which of them will melt faster than the others.

DANCING BEARS

Part of the fun at the big New Year's party in Moscow is being entertained by actors dressed as dancing bears. Let the children make little hats by decorating paper cups with stickers, yarn, glitter, etc. Glue a cotton ball on top of each hat and attach yarn ties to the sides. Help the children put on their hats and have them sit on the floor in a circle. Then let two or three children at a time dance in the middle of the circle while everyone sings the song below.

Sung to: "The Mulberry Bush"

Here come the dancing bears,
Dancing bears, dancing bears.
Here come the dancing bears,
All around the ring.

See them stand up on two legs,
On two legs, on two legs.
See them stand up on two legs,
All around the ring.

See them jump and clap their hands,
Clap their hands, clap their hands.
See them jump and clap their hands,
All around the ring.

Goodbye, little dancing bears,
Dancing bears, dancing bears.
Goodbye, little dancing bears,
We like the way you dance.

Jean Warren

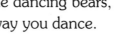

ICE SKATING

Let the children wear their fur hats from the Art activity on p. 11 while they enjoy this version of ice skating. Have them take off their shoes and pretend to put on ice skates. Then play music and let them "skate" in their stocking feet on a bare waxed floor. To make the sliding and gliding easier, sprinkle some cornmeal on the floor first.

BALLET DANCING

Let the children dance to music from a Russian ballet such as "The Nutcracker" or "Swan Lake." Encourage them to try dancing on their tiptoes and to move their arms and bodies gracefully in time to the music. If desired, tell the children a little about the story of the ballet so they can act out the various roles as they dance.

MUSIC

TROIKA, TROIKA
Sung to: "Twinkle, Twinkle, Little Star"

Troika *(troy-kah),* troika, one, two, three.
Troika, troika, please pull me
Over ice and over snow,
Ringing sleigh bells as we go.
Troika, troika, one, two, three.
Troika, troika, please pull me.

Have the children line up as if riding in a sleigh. Then let three children at a time be the troika (three-horse team) and lead the other children around the room while everyone sings the song.

Elizabeth McKinnon

DANCE, LITTLE SNOW GIRL
Sung to: "Ten Little Indians"

Dance, dance, dance, little Snow Girl,
Dance, dance, dance, little Snow Girl,
Dance, dance, dance, little Snow Girl.
Dance in your little red boots.

Additional verses: "Skip, little Snow Girl; Twirl, little Snow Girl; Hop, little Snow Girl; Jump, little Snow Girl." Let the children pretend to put on little red boots before singing the song.

Jean Warren

NEW YEAR'S TREATS

Fill plastic sandwich bags with nuts, raisins and other dried fruits. Seal each bag by stapling a folded piece of colored construction paper over the top. Decorate the construction paper with snowman stickers (or snowman pictures cut from wrapping paper) and glitter. Then choose two children to be Grandfather Frost and Snow Girl and let them hand out the treats while wishing everyone a Happy New Year.

CABBAGE SOUP

On New Year's Day, Russian families and their guests enjoy a variety of delicious foods. Let the children celebrate by helping to make a Russian favorite — cabbage soup. Bring a pot of beef broth to a boil. Then shred some cabbage and slice a few carrots and a bunch of green onions. Add the vegetables to the broth, salt to taste, then cover and simmer for about 40 minutes or until the vegetables are tender. Pour the soup into small bowls and top with spoonfuls of plain yogurt, if desired. Serve with slices of pumpernickel or rye bread.

SNOW GIRL

A Russian Folktale Adapted by Elizabeth McKinnon

Long ago in a forest lived an old man and his wife. They had a cozy little house and some hens and a rooster. But they were lonely because they had no children.

One cold winter day the old man and his wife made a little girl out of snow to keep them company. "See how pretty she is," said the old woman. "How I wish she were a real child."

Then a wonderful thing happened. As the old couple watched, the snow girl turned into a real little girl with golden curls and sparkling blue eyes! When she spoke, her voice was soft and gentle. "May I please stay and live with you?" she asked.

The old man and his wife were overjoyed. "Of course you may stay with us," they said. They named their new child Snow Girl and gave her a fur cap and a pair of little red boots.

The old man and his wife loved Snow Girl. She was a happy child who was always laughing and singing. But she didn't like to stay indoors for very long. "I must not get too warm," she would say. Then she would run outside in her little red boots to dance and skip among the soft twirling snowflakes.

As time went by, the days grew warmer. The ice on the rivers began to melt and a few blades of grass pushed up through the snow. The other children liked to play in the sunshine. But Snow Girl always played where it was shady and cool.

Then one day it was spring. The sun was shining brightly and all the flowers were in bloom. Snow Girl put her arms around the old man and his wife. "It's time for me to leave now," she said. "I must go to the Far North and live for awhile with Grandfather Frost. But don't be sad. I'll always come back to stay with you in wintertime."

The old man and his wife were sorry to see Snow Girl go. But she kept her promise. Every year when the first snowflakes began to fall she came back to spend the winter with the old man and his wife, and that made them very happy indeed.

Chinese New Year

A Chinese Celebration

CHINESE NEW YEAR
A Chinese Celebration

For children in China, the biggest and most exciting holiday of the year is New Year's. The celebration takes place in January or February and lasts for fifteen days.

Before New Year's Day the children help their families sweep and scrub their houses clean. Rooms are decorated with red and pink flowers and with red scrolls that wish everyone happiness and prosperity in the coming year. Red is thought to be a lucky color, so it is seen everywhere during the holiday.

On New Year's Day the festivities begin. Shops and businesses close and families gather together to celebrate. The children dress in their best clothes and wear new shoes. For New Year's presents they receive little red envelopes of "lucky money" that they can use later to buy holiday treats.

Throughout the day the children are on their best behavior, for they know that saying and doing nice things will bring good fortune in the new year. In the evening, after eating a special dinner, they spend time with their families playing games, singing songs and listening to stories.

As the holiday continues, the children and their parents pay New Year's visits, taking along gifts of tangerines or oranges. In the streets the noise of firecrackers is everywhere. Musicians play drums and cymbals while dancers, holding up a brightly painted lion head with a long cloth attached to the back, dance and weave through the crowds of people. The children love to tease the fierce-looking lion as it chases away "evil spirits."

The New Year's celebration ends with the Lantern Festival. On that night a giant dragon made of silk and bamboo is carried through the streets while the children and their families follow along holding lighted paper lanterns.

NEW YEAR'S SCROLL

Make a scroll with the children to hang in your room for a Chinese New Year's decoration. For a background use a long piece of red wrapping paper or sheets of red construction paper taped together. Use a black felt-tip marker to write "Gung Hay Fat Choy" (Happy New Year) in the center of the paper. Then set out a variety of red and pink materials (yarn, fabric scraps, ribbon, buttons, magazine pictures, glitter, etc.) and let the children glue them around the New Year's message. When they have finished, glue the ends of the paper around long cardboard tubes and hang the scroll on a wall or a bulletin board.

CHINESE FANS

On a clean tabletop have the children brush water on thin paper plates and smooth them flat with their hands. Allow the plates to dry. Then let the children brush diluted glue on their plates and place precut red and pink tissue paper flower shapes on top of the glue. Make a handle for each fan by gluing two tongue depressors together and slipping the edge of the paper plate in between them while the glue is still wet.

LUCKY MONEY PRIZE GAMES

Tape pennies to the centers of red construction paper squares. Have the children fold the edges of the papers over the pennies and seal them with gold or yellow stickers to make "lucky money envelopes." Let the children play card games such as Lotto or Concentration. (The idea of using cards to play games originated in China.)

When the games are over, place the lucky money envelopes in a paper bag. Then let each child reach in and take out a prize.

LANGUAGE

CHINESE ANIMAL ZODIAC

In China each new year is named for one of the twelve animals in the zodiac cycle. For example, 1984 was the Year of the Mouse and 1987 was the Year of the Rabbit. It is believed that the year in which a person is born determines his or her characteristics. Use the chart at the right to find the animal name of your celebration year. Then locate the children's birth years on the chart and discuss their animal signs. Talk about the other animals, too, and let the children act out their movements. Follow up by singing the song "Here Come the New Years" on p. 25.

Mouse	1948	1960	1972	1984	1996
Cow	1949	1961	1973	1985	1997
Tiger	1950	1962	1974	1986	1998
Rabbit	1951	1963	1975	1987	1999
Dragon	1952	1964	1976	1988	2000
Snake	1953	1965	1977	1989	2001
Horse	1954	1966	1978	1990	2002
Sheep	1955	1967	1979	1991	2003
Monkey	1956	1968	1980	1992	2004
Rooster	1957	1969	1981	1993	2005
Dog	1958	1970	1982	1994	2006
Pig	1959	1971	1983	1995	2007

STORYTIME FUN

Read or tell the Chinese folktale "Little Fox and the Tiger" on p. 27. When the children have become familiar with the story, let them take turns acting out the roles of the animal characters.

22

GROWING BEAN SPROUTS

Let the children help grow bean sprouts to eat as part of their New Year's snacks or to enjoy later in salads or sandwiches. Put ⅓ cup mung beans (available at supermarkets and health food stores) in a quart jar and soak them in water overnight. The next day use an ice pick to punch about ten holes in the jar lid, making sure that the holes are smaller than the beans. Screw on the jar lid and drain the beans. Then rinse and drain them again. Place the jar at an angle so that the water will continue to drain and cover the jar with a towel. Over the next four to six days let the children help rinse and drain the beans, once in the early morning and once in the late afternoon. Keep the jar covered with the towel between rinsings. When the sprouts are about 1½ inches long, rinse them in a bowl of water to remove the hulls. Use them right away or store them in a refrigerator for up to a week.

CHOW MEIN

Celebrate Chinese New Year by setting the snack table with red placemats and napkins. Prepare canned *chow mein* according to the directions on the label and add some fresh bean sprouts, if desired (see Science activity above). Serve on top of rice or crunchy Chinese noodles and set out soy sauce for tasting. For dessert give each child two tangerine or orange segments (two is a lucky number).

Extension: Traditionally, everyone in China has a birthday on New Year's Day no matter when he or she was born. Let the children observe this custom by singing "Happy Birthday" to themselves after enjoying their snacks.

EGG FLOWER SOUP

Pour 3 cups chicken broth into a saucepan and bring to a boil over medium heat. In a small jar with a lid, shake together 1 tablespoon cornstarch and 2 tablespoons cold water. Pour the cornstarch mixture into the broth and stir until smooth. Beat 1 egg with a fork in a small bowl. Then drop spoonfuls of the beaten egg into the broth and stir, letting the children watch as the egg forms into shreds, or "flowers." When the egg is completely cooked, pour the soup into small bowls and sprinkle with chopped green onion "leaves." Makes 6 small servings.

RIBBON DANCING

As part of your New Year's celebration, try this version of Chinese ribbon dancing. Attach colorful ribbons or crepe paper streamers to cardboard tubes or tongue depressors. Let the children hold the ribbons while dancing to recordings of Chinese songs or other rhythmic music. Encourage them to move their ribbons in large and small circles, in figure eights, up and down like waves and in swirls above their heads.

LION DANCE PARADE

Let the children help decorate a cardboard box (about 12 inches square) to make a lion head. On one side of the box glue construction paper facial features and a fringed beard. Attach crepe paper streamers to the top of the box and a long piece of cloth to the back. Cut hand holes in the sides of the box near the bottom. Let one child at a time hold the lion head above his or her head while one or two other children get under the cloth and hang on behind. Then play library recordings of Chinese music (or use any appropriate music) and let the children have a Lion Dance Parade. As the lion prances, sways and shakes its head, have the other children follow along behind playing drums, cymbals and other rhythm instruments.

HERE COME THE NEW YEARS
Sung to: "Old MacDonald Had a Farm"

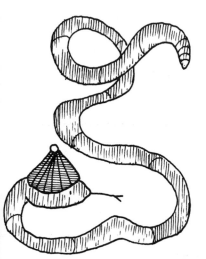

Here come the new years
Marching round, E-I-E-I-O.
And one of the years
Is the Year of the Mouse, E-I-E-I-O.
With a squeak, squeak here,
And a squeak, squeak there,
Here a squeak, there a squeak,
Everywhere a squeak, squeak.
Here come the new years
Marching round, E-I-E-I-O.

Sing a verse of the song for each Chinese zodiac animal:
"Year of the Cow - moo, moo; Tiger - grrr, grrr; Rabbit - sniff, sniff;
Dragon - roar, roar; Snake - hiss, hiss; Horse - neigh, neigh;
Sheep - baa, baa; Monkey - chee, chee; Rooster - cock-a-doodle;
Dog - bow-wow; Pig - oink, oink."

Elizabeth McKinnon

LION DANCE SONG
Sung to: "Mary Had a Little Lamb"

See the lion dance and prance,
Dance and prance, dance and prance.
See the lion dance and prance
On Chinese New Year's Day.

Hear the firecrackers pop,
Pop, pop, pop; pop, pop, pop.
Hear the firecrackers pop
On Chinese New Year's Day.

Additional verses: "Hear the drums go boom, boom,
boom; Hear the cymbals clang, clang, clang; See the
children laugh and clap."

Elizabeth McKinnon

CHINESE HELLO SONG
Sung to: "The Farmer in the Dell"

Let's wave and say "Ni hao (nee how),"
Let's wave and say "Ni hao."
Let's say "hello" to all our friends,
Let's wave and say "Ni hao."

Explain to the children that *ni hao* is the Chinese way of
saying "hello."

Elizabeth McKinnon

LITTLE FOX AND THE TIGER
A Chinese Folktale Adapted by Elizabeth McKinnon

One day Little Fox was playing by herself in the forest when suddenly a tiger jumped out from behind a tree.

"Yum, yum," said the tiger. "I'm going to eat you up!"

Little Fox was frightened, but she kept her wits about her. In no time at all she had thought of a plan.

"I'm sorry, Mr. Tiger, but you can't eat me up," she said.

"And why not?" asked the tiger in surprise.

"Because I am very important," said Little Fox. "In fact, I am ruler of this forest. All the other animals are so afraid of me, they run away when I walk by."

The tiger was suspicious. "How can I be sure you are telling the truth?" he asked.

"That's easy," said Little Fox. "You follow behind me as I walk through the forest. Then you will see for yourself how important I am."

So Little Fox started off with the tiger walking behind her.

Soon they came across a deer playing among the trees. When the deer saw Little Fox, he paid no attention to her at all. But when he saw the tiger, he ran off into the bushes just as Little Fox thought he would.

"You see?" said Little Fox. "That deer is very afraid of me."

Next, Little Fox and the tiger came upon a wolf sitting outside his cave. Again, the wolf paid no attention to Little Fox. But when he saw the tiger walking behind her, he jumped up and ran inside his cave to hide.

"You see? " said Little Fox. "Even that big wolf is afraid of me."

Little Fox and the tiger continued on their way. Before long they came to a riverbank where a bear was fishing. Usually the bear was not afraid of anybody. He hardly even noticed Little Fox. But when he saw the tiger, he jumped into the river with a big splash and swam away as fast as he could.

"Now do you believe me?" asked Little Fox.

The tiger was completely fooled. He bowed down and said, "Forgive me, Little Fox. I had no idea you were so important. From now on I'll never bother you again."

So Little Fox went back to playing in the forest, feeling very pleased with herself for thinking of such a good trick.

Doll's Day
and Boy's Day

Japanese Children's Celebrations

DOLL'S DAY AND BOY'S DAY
Japanese Children's Celebrations

Spring is a happy time for children in Japan. They have two festivals to celebrate — Doll's Day and Boy's Day.

DOLL'S DAY

Hina Matsuri, or Doll's Day, falls on March 3. On that day girls invite their friends over for tea parties to see their special Doll's Day dolls, which represent the Emperor and Empress and members of their court. The dolls, dressed in rich brocaded robes, are often handed down from mother to daughter and are not meant to be played with. Instead, they are displayed on a stand that is built like a staircase and covered with a bright red cloth. The Emperor and Empress dolls are placed on the top shelf with the other dolls arranged on the lower shelves. On the bottom shelf are miniature pieces of furniture and household articles such as tiny chests of drawers, candle stands and little sets of lacquered dinnerware.

At the tea parties guests play games with their everyday dolls, which they have brought with them to enjoy the fun. And when it's time for refreshments, the girls use their best manners to offer candies and cakes to their dolls before eating the sweets themselves.

When Doll's Day is over, the special stand is taken down. Then the girls help pack their Doll's Day dolls in boxes and store them away until the following year.

BOY'S DAY

Boy's Day, officially called Children's Day, is celebrated on May 5, and the symbol for this holiday is the *koi* (carp). In each family the boys help their father erect a tall bamboo pole outside the house. Then together they hang colorful cloth or paper carp on the pole, with the largest one at the top for the oldest son and the smaller ones beneath it for the younger brothers. When the carp fill out in the wind, they appear to be swimming and leaping just like real fish.

According to legend, the carp was chosen to symbolize Boy's Day because of its ability to swim up streams and waterfalls. The carp's determination to overcome all obstacles was thought to be a good example for young boys to follow.

Note: Although traditionally, Doll's Day is for girls and Boy's Day is for boys, be sure to include all of your children in both celebrations.

DOLL'S DAY ACTIVITIES

ART

TISSUE CHERRY BLOSSOMS

For your Doll's Day celebration let the children make cherry blossom pictures to decorate a wall or a bulletin board. Use a brown crayon to draw bare branches on pieces of light blue construction paper. Hand out the papers along with sheets of pink facial tissue. Let the children tear the facial tissue into tiny pieces. Then have them spread small circles of glue on their branches and press bits of tissue all over the glue to create fluffy blossoms.

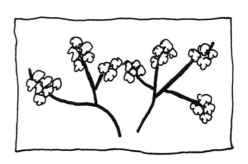

Note: This activity also can be used to make peach blossoms — the flowers traditionally associated with Doll's Day.

JAPANESE PAPER FOLDING

Let the children try this version of *origami* (Japanese paper folding). Cut 5-inch circles out of origami paper (available at art stores or Asian import shops) or out of different kinds of brightly colored wrapping paper. Set out the circles along with sheets of white construction paper, felt-tip markers and glue. Let the children fold the circles into any shapes they wish and glue them on their papers. Then let them turn their shapes into dolls, flowers, animals, etc., by adding details with felt-tip markers.

Variation: If desired, let the children fold squares rather than circles of paper.

SNACKS

DOLL'S DAY PARTY

The traditional treats for Doll's Day are pastel colored candies and rice cakes. For a sugarless alternative use canape or small cookie cutters to cut shapes out of bread slices. In separate bowls whip cream cheese with small amounts of fruit juice and add drops of food coloring to create pastel shades. Spread the cheese on the bread shapes and arrange them on small paper plates. Serve with tea and thin melon slices, if desired. For added fun make tables by placing cardboard boxes upside down on the floor and setting them with colorful placemats. Then let the children take off their shoes and sit around the tables while enjoying their Doll's Day snacks.

DOLL'S DAY STAND

Arrange cardboard boxes to make a staircase-like stand and cover it with red crepe paper or cloth. (Or attach red paper to a wall and place a table covered with red paper against it.) Invite each child to bring in a favorite doll or toy to display on the Doll's Day stand. You also could bring in a doll or a figurine that means something special to you. When the display is ready, have the children gather around the stand and take turns telling something about the dolls or toys they brought. If desired, start the discussion by telling a little story about your own doll or figurine.

Variation: Use the display to explore spatial relationships by asking questions such as these: "Which dolls are on the top of the stand? Which toys are on the bottom? Which doll is next to the teddy bear? Which toy is in front of the baby doll?"

═══════════ **MUSIC** ═══════════

HINA MATSURI SONG

Sung to: "London Bridge"

Kyō wa tanoshii,
(kyo-oh wa-ah tah-no-shee)
Tanoshii, tanoshii.
(tah-no-shee, tah-no-shee)
Kyō wa tanoshii.
(kyo-oh wa-ah tah-no-shee)
Hina Matsuri!
(hee-nah mah-tsu-ree)

Today is such a happy day,
Happy day, happy day.
Today is such a happy day.
It's Doll's Day today!

Elizabeth McKinnon

═══════════ **MOVEMENT** ═══════════

DANCING DOLLS

Let the children pretend to be Doll's Day dolls that have been packed away in their boxes for the year. Have them lie down on the floor. Then play library recordings of Japanese music (or use any appropriate music) to signal that Doll's Day has arrived. Have the "dolls" hop up out of their boxes and dance as long as they hear the music. Whenever the music stops, have them get back down into their boxes and lie still. Continue starting and stopping the music as long as interest lasts.

BOY'S DAY ACTIVITIES

ART

BOY'S DAY CARP

Use a white paper sack to make a *koi* (carp) for each child. Cut a large circle out of the bottom of the sack for the fish's mouth and cut scallops along the open end to make a tail. Draw large black circles on the sides of the sack for eyes. Let the children use felt-tip markers to decorate their paper fish. Then let them glue colorful strips of tissue paper or crepe paper on their fish's tails. When they have finished, punch two holes in the bottom of each sack (in the corners above the mouth) and tie a piece of string

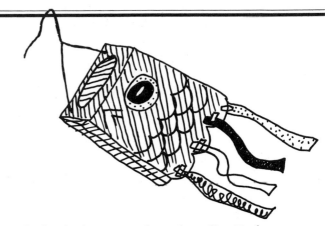

through the holes to make a handle. Before hanging the fish on a pole or from the ceiling, let the children take them outside and move them in the wind like kites.

LEARNING GAMES

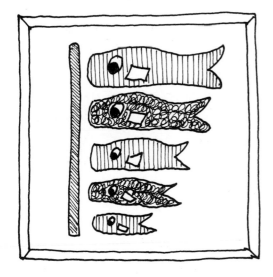

FLANNELBOARD FISH GAME

Cut five fish shapes out of colored felt, making each one bigger than the one before it. Place a long piece of brown yarn on the flannelboard to represent an upright pole. Then let the children take turns arranging the fish shapes down the side of the pole from largest to smallest.

Variation: Let each child place fish shapes down the pole to represent the children in his or her family, starting with a large fish for the oldest child at the top. (Cut out additional fish shapes beforehand, if necessary.)

LANGUAGE

STORYTIME FUN

Read or tell the Japanese folktale "Little Bunny and the Crocodile" on p. 37. Talk about the trick that Little Bunny played. Then tape green construction paper crocodile shapes on the floor for the children to hop across and count.

BOY'S DAY GOLDFISH

For your Boy's Day celebration bring in a goldfish, a goldfish bowl, aquarium gravel, aquarium plants and fish food. Explain to the children that goldfish are members of the carp family and that Japanese children often keep goldfish as pets. Fill the goldfish bowl with treated water (check pet store for instructions) and let the children help add the aquarium gravel and the plants before placing the goldfish in its new home. Then set the goldfish bowl on the science table and discuss care and feeding instructions.

Variation: Take a field trip to a pet shop and let the children choose a goldfish to bring back for your room. Ask the salesperson to explain how to feed and care for it.

MUSIC

BOY'S DAY SONG
Sung to: "The Farmer in the Dell"

My fish is up so high,
My fish is up so high.
Oh my, just watch it fly,
My fish is up so high.

My fish is falling down,
My fish is falling down.
Oh no, it's down so low,
My fish is falling down.

The wind has caught my fish,
The wind has caught my fish.
What fun, I'm on the run,
The wind has caught my fish.

Tie crepe paper streamers around the children's wrists. Then divide the children into groups and let them take turns acting out the movements of the fish while everyone else sings. (If desired, substitute the word *koi* (koy) for "fish" when singing the song.)

Jean Warren

JAPANESE NOODLES

One of the most favorite snacks in Japan is a bowl of hot noodles. You can buy the authentic instant variety (called *ramen*) at many large supermarkets or at Asian food stores. Cook the noodles according to the package directions and serve in small bowls. Then let the children sprinkle on chopped toppings such as hard-boiled eggs, green onions, mushrooms or celery. One package of instant ramen makes 2 to 3 small servings.

Hint: Because the noodles are quite long, you may wish to break them up before cooking.

RICE CRACKERS AND TEA

For a quick and *easy* snack serve Japanese rice crackers (called *sembei*) and green tea. (Both are available at some large supermarkets or at Asian food stores.) Green tea is enjoyed by everyone in Japan, including the children.

LITTLE BUNNY AND THE CROCODILE

A Japanese Folktale Adapted by Jean Warren

Once upon a time Little Bunny lived all by herself on a small island. Since she had no other rabbits to play with, she was very lonely.

Across the water was a big island that was filled with rabbits. Little Bunny spent her days watching the other rabbits and wishing that somehow she could get over to the big island.

One day Little Bunny saw a crocodile on the beach. His nice broad back gave Little Bunny an idea. "I will trick Mr. Crocodile into helping me get to the big island," she thought.

Little Bunny hopped up to the crocodile and said, "Mr. Crocodile, you swim all day in the water and I play all day on my island, so we don't know much about each other. I wonder which one of us has the most friends."

"Oh, I have the most friends," said the crocodile. "You can't see them now because they've all gone for a swim."

"If you lined up all your friends, would they reach as far as the big island?" asked Little Bunny.

"Yes, indeed," said the crocodile. "I will show you."

The crocodile swam off in search of the other crocodiles. When he returned, he lined up his crocodile friends between the big island the small island.

"Oh, you do have many friends," said Little Bunny. "But just to make sure you have more friends than I do, I'd better count them."

Little Bunny hopped onto the back of the first crocodile. Then she began to count by hopping from the back of one crocodile to the back of the next. "One, two, three, four, five, six, seven, eight."

When Little Bunny reached the last crocodile, she hopped off onto the shore of the big island. Soon she was surrounded by many new rabbit friends.

When the crocodile swam over to the big island, he was very surprised. "You have a lot of friends, too, Little Bunny," he said. "I will count them. One, two, three, four, five, six, seven, eight, nine, ten!"

The crocodile smiled. "I was wrong, Little Bunny," he said. "You are the one who has the most friends. You are a very lucky little bunny."

"Yes, I am!" said Little Bunny. And off she hopped.

Saint Patrick's Day

An Irish Celebration

SAINT PATRICK'S DAY
An Irish Celebration

Saint Patrick's Day, celebrated on March 17, is "a great day for the Irish" both in Ireland and in the United States.

Because the holiday honors Saint Patrick, who first brought Christianity to Ireland, Irish families start the day by going to church. Children and adults alike wear sprigs of shamrocks. According to legend, Saint Patrick used the shamrock to teach the meaning of the Trinity, which is why the three-leaved plant became the holiday symbol.

After church there are special Saint Patrick's Day programs and plays for the children to attend. And almost everywhere they can watch Saint Patrick's Day parades and buy pots of shamrocks at little street stalls. As the day goes on, the festivities continue with music, singing and the dancing of Irish jigs.

In the United States, too, Saint Patrick's Day is celebrated with much merrymaking. Everyone joins in "the wearing of the green." In New York and other large cities, children and adults line the streets to watch Saint Patrick's Day parades. They wear green hats and wave Irish flags as the marching bands pass by playing tunes such as "MacNamara's Band" and "When Irish Eyes Are Smiling." Sometimes green lines are painted down the middle of the streets, and there are always people dressed in imaginative green costumes to entertain the crowds. Afterward, families and friends usually get together to continue celebrating with Saint Patrick's Day parties.

LEPRECHAUN LADDERS

Let the children make "leprechaun ladders" to use as room decorations for Saint Patrick's Day. Cut white or clear plastic straws into 1-inch sections. Cut 3-inch shamrock shapes out of green construction paper and punch holes in the centers (make sure that the holes are smaller than the ends of the straw sections). Give each child ten shamrock shapes, nine straw sections and a 2-foot length of green yarn with a straw section tied at one end and the other end taped to make a "needle." Then let the children string their shamrock shapes on their pieces of yarn with a straw section between each shamrock. When they have finished, hang their leprechaun ladders from the ceiling or in a window.

Hint: For a fun surprise, sprinkle a light dusting of flour on the shamrocks for the children to discover on Saint Patrick's Day morning. Explain that the "magic dust" was left by leprechauns as they climbed and danced on their ladders!

SAINT PATRICK'S DAY HATS

Make a hat for each child out of a paper plate. Cut the plate halfway through, roll it into a cone shape to fit the child's head and tape the edges in place. Set out glue and a variety of green materials (felt-tip markers, crepe paper strips, shamrock stickers, glitter, etc.). Then let the children use the materials to decorate their hats any way they wish. When they have finished, attach green yarn to the sides of the hats for ties.

POTATO HOP

In Ireland farmers start planting their potato crops on Saint Patrick's Day. Let the children honor the Irish potato by playing this counting game. Cut ten large potato shapes out of brown construction paper and number them from 1 to 10. Tape the shapes to the floor in the proper sequence. Then let the children take turns hopping from one potato to the other as everyone recites the rhyme below. (When it's time to stop the game, change the last line of the rhyme to read: "Now let's *not* start over again.")

> One potato, two potato,
> Three potato, four,
> Five potato, six potato,
> Seven potato, more.
> Eight potato, nine potato,
> Here is ten.
> Now let's start all over again.

Adapted Traditional

═══ **SCIENCE** ═══

SPROUT SHAMROCKS

Start this activity about one week before Saint Patrick's Day if you want green shamrocks for your celebration. Cut a shamrock shape for each child out of terrycloth. Have the children place their shamrocks in aluminum pie tins and add a little water. Then let them sprinkle alfalfa seeds all over their shapes. Place the pie tins in a sunny spot and have the children regularly add water to keep the shapes moist. Let them observe during the week as the seeds sprout and turn their shamrocks green.

STORYTIME FUN

Read or tell the Irish folktale "The Little Old Lady and the Leprechaun" on p. 47. Discuss leprechauns and how they like to play tricks on people. Then let the children play "Find the Pot of Gold." Cut five squares out of red construction paper to make "scarves." On one of the squares, use crayons to draw a black pot full of gold pieces. Place the squares around the room with the pot-of-gold square face down. Let the children take turns picking up a square. If the square is blank, have the child put it back where it was before. When a child picks up the pot-of-gold square, offer congratulations for "outsmarting the leprechaun." Then have the child exchange the pot-of-gold square with one of the blank squares while the other children cover their eyes. Have the child sit out the game until the pot-of-gold square is turned up again.

LEPRECHAUN, LEPRECHAUN

Recite the poem below and let the children fill in the blanks with names of green things (or have them name things they see around them that are green).

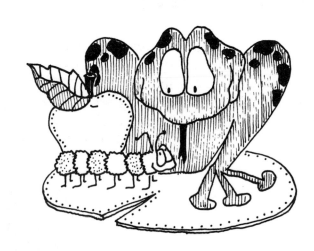

Leprechaun, leprechaun,
Come hunt with me.
How many green things can we see?
We found a green (leaf/etc.) under a tree.
We found a green (frog/etc.) next to me.
We found a green (apple/etc.) on the ground.
We found green (caterpillars/etc.) all around.

Jean Warren

SAINT PATRICK'S DAY PARADE

Help the children put on their Saint Patrick's Day hats from the Art activity on p. 41 and tie green crepe paper streamers around their waists. Then play library recordings of Irish music (or use any appropriate music) and let the children parade around the room while playing rhythm instruments. If desired, tape a line of green crepe paper or yarn to the floor for the children to follow as they march.

SHAMROCK SEARCH

Cut shamrock shapes out of green felt and hide them around the room. Then let the children search for the shapes while singing the song at the right. Each time they find a shamrock, have them place it on the flannelboard and take a bow. When all the shamrocks have been found, count them together with the children.

Sung to: "The Farmer in the Dell"

Let's look for shamrocks now,
Let's look for shamrocks now,
And when we find a bright green one,
Then we can take a bow!

Jean Warren

IF YOU'RE WEARING GREEN TODAY
Sung to: "If You're Happy and You Know It"

If you're wearing green today, dance a jig,
If you're wearing green today, dance a jig.
If you're wearing green today,
Dance a jig, then smile and say,
"Have a very Happy Saint Patrick's Day!"

Additional verses: "If you're wearing green today, clap your hands; If you're wearing green today, twirl around; If you're wearing green today, shout 'Hurray!'"

Elizabeth McKinnon

LEPRECHAUNS

Sung to: "Three Blind Mice"

Leprechauns, leprechauns,
Hiding here, hiding there.
They don't want us to see them play
When they come out on Saint Patrick's Day.
See them smile in their cute little way,
Leprechauns, leprechauns.

**Margery A. Kranyik
Hyde Park, MA**

A LITTLE GREEN MAGIC

For each child place 1 tablespoon instant pistachio pudding mix in a baby food jar. Add 2 tablespoons cold milk and watch as the contents turn green. Put lids securely on the jars and have the children shake them for about 45 seconds. Then let the children eat their pudding snacks with small spoons. What makes the pudding turn green? "Leprechaun magic," of course!

**Lisa Fransen
Tucson, AZ**

IRISH SODA BREAD

Let the children help make this Irish treat for your Saint Patrick's Day celebration. In a large bowl mix together 2 cups sifted flour, 3 teaspoons baking soda and ½ teaspoon salt. Use fingers to blend in ¼ cup butter or margarine. Stir in 1 cup milk and add ½ cup raisins or currants. Knead the dough briefly, then shape into a flat loaf and place in a greased pie tin. Bake at 350 degrees for 30 to 35 minutes. Cut into wedges and serve warm with butter.

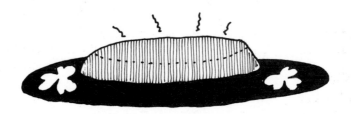

THE LITTLE OLD LADY AND THE LEPRECHAUN

An Irish Folktale Adapted by Elizabeth McKinnon

One day a little old lady was out walking when she heard a tiny little sound.

Tap, tap, tap. Tap, tap, tap.

"I wonder what that could be," said the little old lady.

She peeked behind a nearby tree. And there, to her surprise, she saw a leprechaun dressed all in green. He was tapping away with his little hammer, making shoes for the wee folk to wear.

The little old lady grabbed hold of the leprecaun's coat. "I've caught you now, Mr. Leprechaun!" she cried.

"Indeed you have," said the leprechaun calmly. "But I'll thank you to let me go so I can get on with my work."

"Oh, no," said the little old lady. "Not until you tell me where to find your gold. Everyone knows that when a leprechaun is caught, he has to show where his pot of gold is buried."

The leprechaun chuckled. "So, you want my pot of gold, do you? Very well. Just follow me and I'll show you."

The leprechaun started off with the little old lady holding tight to his coattails.

At last they came to a field where hundreds of bushes were growing. The leprechaun pointed to one of them and said, "Just dig under this bush and you'll find all the gold you want."

The little old lady looked at the hard ground. "I'll have to go home and get a shovel," she said. "But first I'll tie my red scarf on this bush. Then I'll know where to dig when I come back."

"That's a good idea," said the leprechaun with a twinkle in his eye. "Enjoy the gold when you find it!" And with a wave of his hand, he was gone.

The little old lady ran home and got a shovel. As she started back, she began thinking about how she would spend all her gold.

But when she reached the field, her eyes widened in surprise. Instead of one red scarf, she saw hundreds of them. Every single bush had a red scarf tied on it!

"Oh, no!" cried the little old lady. "That leprechaun tricked me! I can't dig under all these bushes. Now I'll have to go home without my pot of gold."

And so she did.

May Day

An English Celebration

MAY DAY
An English Celebration

May 1 has always been a time for May Day festivals in England. The festivals are held locally in small towns and villages where children and adults alike celebrate springtime with age-old customs.

Early in the morning everyone "goes a-Maying" in woods and fields to gather flowers and hawthorn blossoms for the celebration. On the village green a Maypole is set up and decorated with garlands of flowers and long ribbon streamers.

Around noon the main events of the day begin. Everyone gathers to greet the May Queen, who has been chosen from among the girls in the village. The children carry bouquets of spring flowers as they help escort the May Queen and her attendants through the village in a festive procession. Sometimes villagers dressed as shepherds and shepherdesses, milkmaids, jesters and other characters join the procession too.

When the procession ends at the village green, the May Queen is crowned with a wreath of flowers. Then she watches from her throne as the children and the other villagers dance around the Maypole. At some festivals traditional Morris Dancers join the fun. Wearing bells at their ankles and streamers on their hats and sleeves, the dancers delight the children with their high leaps and jumps.

When the dances are over, there are sports and games for the young people to enjoy. Among the most popular are archery and hoop rolling.

For the children, May Day is not complete without the giving of May baskets. After filling small baskets with flowers, they tiptoe to the doors of friends and leave the baskets on the doorsteps. Then they knock and run away quickly before anyone sees them.

MAY DAY CROWNS

Let every child be a May King or Queen by making a flower crown to wear for your celebration. Cut the centers out of paper plates and have the children paint the rims green. When the paint has dried, let the children crumple small circles cut from various colors of tissue paper and glue them on their plate rims for flowers. Then let them glue short strips of colored tissue paper or crepe paper around the edges of their crowns.

Variation: Let the children decorate their crowns by poking dandelions or other flowers through slits cut in their green plate rims.

MAY BASKETS

Cut 9-inch circles (one for every two children) out of pastel colored construction paper and cut the circles in half. Cut 9-inch strips from matching colored construction paper to use for handles. Give each of the children a half-circle and let them use crayons or flower stickers to decorate their papers. When they have finished, roll each half-circle into a cone shape and staple the edges together. Then use tape or glue to attach handles. Let the children fill their baskets with real or artificial flowers or with flowers made from construction paper.

Variation: For a lacy touch fold a 5-inch paper doily in half over the straight edge of each half-circle before rolling it into a cone shape and stapling it.

STORYTIME FUN

Read or tell the English folktale "Lazy Jack" on p. 57. When the children have become familiar with the story, let them use improvised props to act out the roles of the characters.

NURSERY RHYMES

Nursery rhymes, which originated in England, are naturals for teaching language skills. At group time invite the children to recite, sing or act out their favorite rhymes. Then introduce other rhymes that can become new favorites. After reciting a rhyme over several days, pause at the ends of the lines to let the children fill in the rhyming words.

Hint: For your May Day celebration you might want to include the nursery rhyme "Mistress Mary."

> Mistress Mary, quite contrary,
> How does your garden grow?
> With silver bells and cockle shells
> And pretty maids all in a row.

Traditional

═══ LEARNING GAMES ═══

FARMER, FARMER

To review colors, let the children play this outdoor game which is a favorite among English children. Set up two boundary lines (about 15 feet apart) to form a "river." Choose one child to stand in the river and be the Farmer. Have the rest of the children line up along one of the boundary lines and call out, "Farmer, Farmer, may we cross your golden river?" Have the Farmer choose a color and then say, "You can if you're wearing (red/blue/etc.)." Let everyone cross the river to the other side. Those who are wearing the color named can walk slowly, but those who are not must run fast while the Farmer tries to tag them. Have those who are caught stay in the river with the Farmer and help with the tagging during the next round of the game. Continue playing until everyone is standing in the river. Let the last child tagged be the new Farmer.

Hint: Before playing the game, have the children examine their clothing to see what colors they are wearing. Point out that every tiny bit of color counts!

MAY DAY NATURE WALK

Plan to "go a-Maying" with the children as part of your May Day celebration. Take a nature walk to observe the spring plants and flowers. Along the way look for greens, dandelions and other wildflowers that the children can pick and take back for their May baskets.

Variation: Visit a florist shop or a nursery to see spring flowers in bloom. If desired, let the children help choose a small flowering plant to buy and take back with you. Encourage them to choose a plant with several buds and ask the salesperson to explain how to care for it.

MAYPOLE DANCING

Make a Maypole by attaching long cloth or crepe paper streamers to a pole or a tree. Add flowers and colorful bows for decorations. Have the children put on their May Day crowns from the Art activity on p. 51 and wear jingle bell bracelets around their ankles, if desired. Then let them hold onto the ends of the streamers and dance around the Maypole while singing the song below.

Sung to: "The Mulberry Bush"

Let's dance around the Maypole today,
Maypole today, Maypole today.
Let's dance around the Maypole today.
We're Kings and Queens of the May.

Elizabeth McKinnon

Variation: For indoor play let the children help make a Maypole decoration by covering a long cardboard tube with green crepe paper and attaching paper flowers, bows and ribbons. Anchor the tube in a tub of clay or playdough and place it on a chair in the center of the room. Then tie crepe paper streamers around the children's wrists and let them dance in a circle around their Maypole decoration.

FLOWER TARGET GAME

Archery is a popular sport at English May Day celebrations. Let the children try this version. On a large piece of paper, draw a target made of three circles, one inside the other. In each circle attach a different kind of flower sticker. Place the target on the floor and have the children line up a few feet away from it. Then let them take turns tossing a beanbag at the target. Whenever a child tosses the beanbag so that it lands inside a circle, give the child a matching flower sticker. Then have the child step out of line and watch as the others take their turns. Continue the game until every child has won a sticker.

Hint: Use age and ability to determine how close the children should stand to the target.

RING AROUND THE ROSIE

Many children's game songs (such as "London Bridge" and "The Mulberry Bush") came to us from England. For your May Day celebration try playing this version of "Ring Around the Rosie." Have the children stand in a circle with one child in the middle. As the children circle round, have them chant the rhyme at the right. When they come to the last line, let the child in the middle of the circle call out a direction for the others to follow: "All touch your toes; All hop on one foot; All clap hands;" etc. Then let the child choose the next person to stand in the middle. Continue playing until everyone has had a turn calling out a direction.

> Ring around the rosie,
> A pocket full of posies.
> Flowers, flowers,
> All (fall down/twirl around/etc.).

Adapted Traditional

MAY DAY SONG

Sung to: "Skip to My Lou"

May Day, May Day, how do you do?
  (Curtsy or bow.)
May Day, May Day, how do you do?
May Day, May Day, how do you do?
Ring the bell and run, run, run.
  (Pretend to ring doorbell, then run in place.)

Leave some flowers for your friends,
  (Pretend to put flowers on doorstep.)
Leave some flowers for your friends,
Leave some flowers for your friends.
Knock, knock, knock and run, run, run.
  (Pretend to knock on door, then run in place.)

Kristine Wagoner
Pacific, WA

MAY DAY'S HERE

Sung to: "London Bridge"

May Day's here with sun so bright,
Sun so bright, sun so bright.
May Day's here with sun so bright.
Hurray for May Day!

May Day's here with flowers in bloom,
Flowers in bloom, flowers in bloom.
May Day's here with flowers in bloom.
Hurray for May Day!

Gayle Bittinger

MAY DAY TEA PARTY

Let the children celebrate May Day with an English tea party. Set the snack table with paper doily placemats and use colorful flowers for decorations. Make tea in a small teapot. When the tea has cooled, let the children take turns pouring small amounts into their cups. Then let them add milk as the English do, if they wish. Serve with toasted crumpets or English muffins and jam.

APPLE FOOL

Fruit fools have always been a favorite sweet in England. (The word "fool" was once used in England as a term of endearment.) Let the children help make this version of apple fool to serve at your tea party. Whip 1 cup whipping cream until it forms stiff peaks. Carefully fold in 1 cup applesauce (see recipe on p. 115) and 1 teaspoon grated lemon rind. Chill thoroughly, then spoon into small cups. Makes 6 small servings.

Variation: Substitute any other pureed canned fruit for the applesauce.

LAZY JACK

An English Folktale Adapted by Elizabeth McKinnon

Once upon a time there was a boy who never did any work at all. People called him Lazy Jack.

One day his mother said, "It's not right for a boy to be so lazy. Tomorrow you must go out and find some work."

So the next day, which was Monday, Jack went to work for a neighbor. When the work was done, the neighbor gave Jack a penny. Jack started for home with the penny in his hand, but along the way he dropped it.

"Silly boy," said his mother. "You should have put it in your pocket."

"I'll do so next time," said Jack.

On Tuesday Jack went to work for a farmer who gave him a little pitcher of milk. Jack remembered what his mother had said. He put the pitcher in his pocket and started off on his way. But as he walked, the milk splashed out of the pitcher. By the time he got home, his clothes were soaking wet and the pitcher was empty.

"Silly boy," said his mother. "You should have carried it on your head."

"I'll do so next time," said Jack.

On Wednesday Jack went to work for a cheesemaker who gave him a soft cream cheese. Jack put the cheese on top of his head and started off on his way. But the sun was very hot. By the time he got home, the cheese had melted down all over his ears and face.

"Silly boy," said his mother. "You should have carried it in your hands."

"I'll do so next time," said Jack.

On Thursday Jack went to work for an old woman who had nothing to give him but a tomcat. Jack picked up the cat and carried it in his hands as he started off on his way. But the cat didn't like that. It scratched Jack's hands so much that he had to let it go.

"Silly boy," said Jack's mother when he got home. "You should have tied it with a string and led it along behind you."

"I'll do so next time," said Jack.

On Friday Jack went to work for a butcher who gave him a leg of lamb. Jack tied a string around the leg of lamb and pulled it behind him as he started on his way. But the ground was all covered with dirt. And by the time Jack got home, the leg of lamb was all covered with dirt too.

"Silly boy," said his mother. "You should have carried it on your shoulder."

"I'll do so next time," said Jack.

On Saturday Jack went to work for a farmer who gave him a donkey. It was hard work, but Jack finally got the donkey up on his shoulders and started off for home.

Along the way he passed a house where a rich man lived with his daughter. The daughter was very beautiful, and she had a pretty smile. But she didn't know how to laugh.

Now the daughter happened to look out the window as Jack walked by with the donkey on his shoulders. It was such a funny sight that she burst out laughing for the very first time in her life. This made her father so happy that he asked Jack to be his daughter's husband.

So the two of them were married and went to live in a fine house. Lazy Jack became very rich and never had to do a day's work again. He invited his mother to come stay in his house, and they all lived happily together.

Lei Day

A Hawaiian Celebration

LEI DAY
A Hawaiian Celebration

May Day is Lei Day in Hawaii. On May 1 children and adults all wear colorful *leis* (garlands of flowers) draped over their shoulders. Leis express the "*aloha* spirit" of Hawaii, which is a spirit of friendship and love.

Lei Day is celebrated everywhere on the islands with lei displays and contests. For the children, there are pageants and programs that include music, singing and *hula* dancing. The hula dancers, wearing leis and grass skirts, gracefully move their hips while acting out the words of songs with their hands. The dancers are accompanied by musicians who play guitars or *ukuleles* or who beat out rhythms with drums, bamboo sticks and gourd rattles. Hula dances tell stories about beautiful things in nature such as the sand and the sea, the warm trade winds, the swaying palms and the mist-covered mountains.

On Lei Day the children may have the chance to attend a *luau* (Hawaiian feast). The luau is held outdoors, and the main dish is a whole roast pig that has been cooked in a pit in the ground. Other foods, such as bananas and yams, are cooked in the pit too. They are served with *poi* (mashed taro root), which guests enjoy eating with their fingers. Topping off the feast are platters of delicious tropical fruits, including mangoes, papayas and fresh pineapple.

TISSUE PAPER LEIS

Cut 3-inch circles, squares and triangles out of different colors of tissue paper and poke holes in the centers. Give each child a piece of yarn about 2 feet long with one end knotted and the other end taped to make a "needle." Then let the children string the tissue paper "flowers" on their pieces of yarn to make leis. When they have finished, tie the leis around the children's necks.

Variation: Make leis by following the directions for "Leprechaun Ladders" on p. 41. Instead of shamrocks, use flower shapes cut from different colors of construction paper.

HAWAIIAN BEACH SCENES

Give the children each a sheet of light blue construction paper. Let them make "beaches" by brushing glue across the bottoms of their papers and sprinkling sand on the glue (use white sand, if available). Then let them glue on small shells and precut sun shapes, palm tree shapes, beach ball shapes, etc., to complete their beach scenes.

PLAYING WITH SEASHELLS

Provide the children with a sandbox and an assortment of seashells. Have them group the shells in the sand by size, kind or color. Or have them line up the shells from smallest to largest. Then let the children experiment with arranging the shells in ways they think up themselves.

TROPICAL FISH PUZZLES

Cut a fish shape for each child out of a large index card or white construction paper and draw on eyes and mouths. Show pictures of tropical fish and discuss their brilliant colors. Let the children use felt-tip markers to decorate their fish shapes with colorful stripes or other designs. When they have finished, cut each child's fish into three puzzle pieces. Then let the children put their own fish back together, using the colors and shapes of the puzzle pieces as guides.

Susan A. Miller
Kutztown, PA

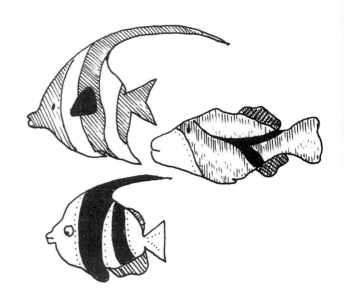

SCIENCE

GROWING A PINEAPPLE PLANT

Let the children help start a pineapple plant to grow in your room. Cut off the leafy top of a fresh pineapple (about 1 inch below the base of the leaves) and scoop out the fruit. Reserve the bottom part of the pineapple to use for the Snack suggestion on p. 65. Place the pineapple top on a plate to dry for several days. Then plant it in a pot of damp sandy soil, leaving the top part of the rind uncovered. Place the plant in a sunny spot and let the children water it regularly. Soon roots will begin to form. If you wait long enough, you might find a little pineapple growing among the green leaves. Meanwhile, you will have an unusual plant in your room to enjoy.

PLANTING PAPAYA SEEDS

If you plan to serve papayas as part of your Hawaiian snacks, save the seeds for planting. Remove the slippery coatings from the seeds, then plant them in a pot of damp soil. Cover the pot loosely with clear plastic wrap and place it in direct sunlight. Check regularly to see that the soil remains moist. Remove the plastic when the seeds begin to sprout.

STORYTIME FUN

Read or tell the Hawaiian folktale "How Maui Made the Sun Slow Down" on p. 67. Then have the children pretend that they are suns and that their arms and legs are rays. Let them walk back and forth across the room showing how they would move across the sky in spring, summer, fall and winter.

Extension: Let the children make "tapa cloth" by brushing water on sheets of white construction paper and crumpling them into balls. Have them smooth out their papers on a flat surface and allow them to dry. Then let them draw designs on their tapa cloth with brown and black felt-tip markers or crayons.

TALKING HULA HANDS

Hula dancers use hand movements to act out the words of songs. With the children make up hand movements for each of these words: "rainbow, waterfall, tree, mountain, sea, flowers, bee, dancers, me." Then recite the poem at the right and let the children use their hand movements to act out the words.

Extension: When the children have become familiar with the hand movements, sing the musical version of the poem on p. 65.

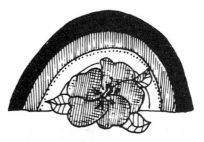

Rainbow over the waterfall,
Rainbow over the tree,
Rainbow over the mountain,
Rainbow over the sea.

Rainbow over the flowers,
Rainbow over the bee,
Rainbow over the dancers,
Rainbow over me!

Jean Warren

HULA HAND PUPPETS

Use brown paper lunch sacks to make hula dancer hand puppets. Cut 5-inch fringes along the open ends of the sacks. Then pass out the flat sacks and help the children draw faces on the bottom parts. Let them glue small flower stickers or bits of colored paper under their hula dancer faces to make leis. Then play library recordings of Hawaiian songs (or use any appropriate music) and let groups of children take turns moving their hand puppets to the music while the others play rhythm instruments.

Variation: Let the children pretend to be hula dancers and dance to the music. Have them wear their leis from the Art activity on p. 61 and use hand movements to act out the words of the songs. If desired, make hula skirts by fringing the open ends of large paper grocery sacks and taping the sacks around the children's waists.

ALOHA SONG
Sung to: "Happy Birthday"

Aloha *(ah-low-ha)* to you,
Aloha to you.
Aloha, hello,
Aloha to you.

Aloha to you,
Aloha to you.
Aloha, goodbye,
Aloha to you.

Elizabeth McKinnon

Explain that *aloha* is the Hawaiian way of saying both "hello" and "goodbye." If desired, let the children place pretend leis over one another's shoulders when they sing each verse of the song. (It's the custom in Hawaii to greet friends who are leaving for a long time or who are returning by giving them leis.)

RAINBOW SONG

Sung to: "Mary Had a Little Lamb"

Rainbow over the waterfall,
Waterfall, waterfall,
Rainbow over the waterfall,
Rainbow over the tree.

Rainbow over the flowers,
Flowers, flowers,
Rainbow over the flowers,
Rainbow over the bee.

Rainbow over the mountain,
Mountain, mountain,
Rainbow over the mountain,
Rainbow over the sea.

Rainbow over the dancers,
Dancers, dancers,
Rainbow over the dancers,
Rainbow over me!

Jean Warren

SNACKS

HAWAIIAN LUAU

Celebrate Lei Day by turning snack time into "luau time." Spread a sheet out on the floor and place paper or artificial flowers in the center for decorations. Let the children help peel and cube tropical fruits such as bananas, papayas, mangoes and fresh pineapple. Arrange the fruits on paper plates and sprinkle on fresh grated coconut, if desired (see recipe below). For poi (mashed taro root) use whipped cream, vanilla yogurt or whipped cream cheese mixed with pineapple juice. Serve in small cups for the children to dip into and eat with their fingers. Then let the children sit around the sheet on the floor and enjoy their snacks while listening to recordings of Hawaiian music.

FRESH GRATED COCONUT

Pass around a coconut for the children to shake and examine. Pierce the eyes of the coconut with an ice pick, drain out the milk and let each child have a taste. Place the coconut on a hard surface and break open the shell with a hammer. Use a strong knife to remove the meat. Peel off the brown skin and cut the meat into pieces. Then let the children help grate the coconut on the fine side of a food grater.

Hint: The meat will be easier to remove from the shell if you bake the coconut at 400 degrees for 15 minutes before breaking it open.

HOW MAUI MADE THE SUN SLOW DOWN

A Hawaiian Folktale Adapted by Elizabeth McKinnon

Long ago there was a boy named Maui who was very strong and brave. He lived with his mother beside a beautiful waterfall.

Maui's mother spent her days making tapa cloth out of mulberry bark. First she soaked the bark in water. Then she pounded the bark into flat sheets on her tapa log. When the tapa cloth was soft and smooth, she laid it out in the sun to dry.

One day Maui's mother said, "How I wish that the days were longer. I start pounding my tapa early in the morning, but by the time I finish the sun is already in the west. Sometimes my tapa cloth never gets dry because the sun moves across the sky so fast."

"I know what to do," said Maui. "I'll find the sun and make him slow down."

That night Maui climbed to the mountaintop where the sun was sleeping inside a deep hole. He found a long vine, and in one end of it he tied a noose. He placed the noose near the edge of the hole where the sun was sleeping. Then he picked up the other end of the vine and hid behind a rock.

Early the next morning the sun woke up and began climbing out of the hole on his long yellow rays. As he did so, one of his rays stepped right in the center of Maui's noose. Maui pulled hard on the other end of the vine, and the noose closed tightly around the sun's ray.

"What is the meaning of this?" roared the sun. "Let me go!"

"Not until you promise to move more slowly across the sky," said Maui. "My mother needs more hours of sunlight to dry her tapa cloth."

"You can't keep me tied up," cried the sun. "Without me, all the plants and animals on earth will die."

"Then let's make a bargain," said Maui. "I will set you free if you promise to go across the sky slowly for part of the year. Then for the rest of the year you can go as fast as you always have."

The sun was very angry, but what could he do? His ray was caught fast in Maui's noose. "All right," he said at last. "I promise."

So Maui set the sun free. Then he hurried home to tell his mother that now she would have more sunlight for drying her tapa cloth.

The sun kept his promise. To this day he still moves fast across the sky in fall and winter. But in spring and summer he travels slowly, giving us long days filled with warmth and sunshine.

Bastille Day

A French Celebration

BASTILLE DAY
A French Celebration

Children in France look forward to July 14, for that is when their country celebrates its most popular holiday — Bastille Day. Bastille Day commemorates France's independence, which makes it similar to America's Fourth of July.

In the morning the children and their families line the streets to watch parades. As the men in uniform and the marching bands pass by, the children wave little French flags, which they have purchased from the many street stalls set up for this special occasion.

The celebrations continue in the afternoon with street fairs and carnivals where the children can enjoy swings and rides. If they live near the seashore, the children may spend the afternoon playing in the sand and watching swimming and boating races. Since bicycling is a popular sport in France, there are sure to be bicycle races to watch or to participate in throughout the country.

But the best part of Bastille Day comes after dark when the skies all over France fill with brilliant fireworks displays. Following the fireworks there is dancing in the streets. Colored lights are strung up around the many small sidewalk cafes where hired musicians provide the music. On this special holiday even the children stay up late to enjoy the festivities, which last far into the night.

OUTDOOR ART SHOW

One of the best known places in Paris is the Left Bank where artists display their pictures in outdoor street stalls. In honor of Bastille Day, turn your yard or playground into a mini Left Bank by holding an outdoor art show. Use tables, easels and outside walls to display the children's artwork or hang pictures from a line with clothespins. Then let the children add to the display by drawing pictures on the sidewalk with colored chalk, weaving colorful yarn through a fence or by creating sculptures with giant discards.

Ellen Javernick
Loveland, CO

Hint: Set up several areas where the children can draw or paint while your art show is in progress. If parents are invited, they will enjoy watching their children at work.

FIREWORKS DISPLAYS

Let the children make pictures of fireworks displays to use as decorations for your Bastille Day celebration. Give them each a large sheet of black construction paper and several small squares cut from colored tissue paper. Have them crumple their squares and glue them in clusters in the centers of their papers. Then let them use Q-Tips to draw lines of glue radiating out from the clusters. While the glue is still wet, have them sprinkle on glitter and shake off the excess.

Sally Horton
Waukegan, IL

Variation: Pour yellow, red and white tempera paint into shallow containers and set out sprigs of parsley, dillweed or Queen Anne's lace (available at florist shops). Then let the children dip the plants into the paint and lightly press them on dark colored construction paper to make prints.

Ann Fair
Uniontown, MD

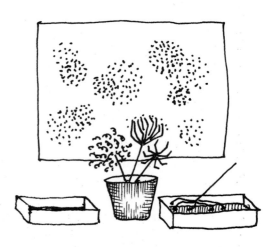

71

COLOR THUMBKIN

Use this version of the French fingerplay "Where Is Thumbkin?" to review colors. Attach different colors of tape or yarn to the fingers of each child's hand. For example, thumb-red, index finger-blue, middle finger-yellow, ring finger-green, little finger-orange. Then sing a verse of the song below for each color.

Sung to: "Frere Jacques"

Where is Red Man, where is Red Man?
> (Hold hand in fist.)

Here I am, here I am.
> (Hold up red finger.)

How are you today, sir?
Very well, I thank you.
> (Bend finger up and down.)

Run away, run away.
> (Put finger behind back.)

Betty Silkunas
Lansdale, PA

SCIENCE

MATCHING SCENTS

France is well-known for its fine perfumes. Discuss how the perfumes are made from flowers that are grown in large fields like crops. After harvesting, the blossoms are pressed to extract the oils that give perfumes their scents. Set out several different kinds of flowers that have strong fragrances (roses, carnations, gardenias, etc.) along with matching scented colognes, soaps or bath salts. Let the children sniff and compare the different fragrances and see if they can match the flowers with their scented products.

BASTILLE DAY BOAT FUN

Let the children make boats by using red and blue crayons to decorate Styrofoam food trays. Make a mast for each boat by poking a pipe cleaner through the center of the tray. Bend the end of the pipe cleaner up under the tray so that the mast will stay in place. Attach red or blue construction paper sails to the pipe cleaners. Then let the children have fun floating and "racing" their Bastille Day boats in a large tub of water.

═══════════ **MOVEMENT** ═══════════

BASTILLE DAY PARADE

Make French flags by dividing 3- by 5-inch index cards into three sections each and coloring the left-hand sections blue and the right-hand sections red (leave the middle sections white). Or let the children use crayons to color the flags, if desired. Staple the flags along the blue edges to plastic straws. Then play marching music (include "*La Marseillaise*," the French national anthem, if possible) and let the children have a Bastille Day Parade. Have them take turns accompanying the music with rhythm instruments while the others follow along behind waving their French flags.

BASTILLE DAY TRIKE FUN

Set up a mini-racecourse on your playground or sidewalk and let the children have a Bastille Day "trike race." Place empty cardboard boxes along the course for the children to go around or in between. Then let them ride trikes on the course one at a time. Explain that the purpose of this kind of race is not to go faster than someone else but to follow the course and finish it.

Hint: For a festive touch decorate the trikes with red, white and blue crepe paper streamers.

FRÈRE JACQUES

Frère Jacques, Frère Jacques,
(fre-ruh jhah-kuh, fre-ruh jhah-kuh)
Dormez-vous, dormez-vous?
(dor-may voo, dor-may voo)
Sonnez les matines,
(so-nay lay mah-tee-nes)
Sonnez les matines,
(so-nay lay mah-tee-nes)
Din, din, don; din, din, don.
(din, din, don; din, din, don)

Are you sleeping, are you sleeping,
Brother John, Brother John?
Morning bells are ringing,
Morning bells are ringing,
Ding, ding, dong; ding, ding, dong.

Traditional

HURRAY FOR BASTILLE DAY
Sung to: "Ten Little Indians"

Fireworks bursting in the night,
  (Open and close hands quickly.)
Watch them make a beautiful sight.
  (Pretend to look through binoculars.)
They give off a sparkling light,
  (Open and close hands quickly.)
Hurray for Bastille Day!
5-4-3-2-1 — BOOM!
  (Jump up with arms and legs extended, then open and close hands slowly while lowering arms.)

Vicki Claybrook
Kennewick, WA

STORYTIME FUN

Read or tell the French folktale "The Silly Wishes" on p. 77. Talk with the children about the woodcutter's silly wishes and how he happened to make them. Then let them each tell what they would have wished for if they had met the elf in the woods.

SNACKS

FRENCH PICNIC

In honor of Bastille Day, plan to have a *pique-nique* (picnic) either outside or indoors. Your menu might include *croissants* or sliced French bread and French cheeses such as *Brie* or *Camembert*. Or mix deviled ham with a little mayonnaise and a dash of Worcestershire sauce to make *pâté*. If desired, serve with grapes or grape juice.

BANANA CRÊPES

For your Bastille Day celebration try making this version of *crêpes* (French pancakes). Use a blender to combine 2 eggs, 1 cup milk, ¾ cup flour, 1 sliced banana, ½ teaspoon salt, ½ teaspoon cinnamon and 2 teaspoons vegetable oil. To make each crêpe, place about 2 tablespoons batter in the center of a hot greased skillet. Tip the pan so that the batter spreads out very thinly. Cook lightly on both sides. Serve the crêpes rolled up with a filling of fresh berries that have been mashed with a small amount of unsweetened frozen apple juice concentrate. Makes 16 to 20 small crêpes.

THE SILLY WISHES
A French Folktale Adapted by Elizabeth McKinnon

Once upon a time a woodcutter lived with his wife in a little house at the edge of a forest.

The woodcutter had everything he needed, but he was always wishing for something more. And he was always grumbling because his wishes never came true. Grumble, grumble, grumble. That's all he did from morning to night.

One day when the woodcutter was working in the forest and grumbling, as usual, an elf popped out from behind a tree.

The woodcutter was very surprised. "Who are you and what do you want?" he asked.

"I am ruler of this forest, and I want some peace and quiet," said the elf. "I'm tired of listening to you grumble all day, so I am going to grant you your next three wishes. Just make sure that you choose them wisely."

The woodcutter was overjoyed. He ran home as fast as he could and told his wife the good news.

"How wonderful!" she cried. "You put some wood on the fire. Then we can sit down and make our three wishes."

So the woodcutter put some logs on the fire, and soon the orange flames were dancing and crackling in the fireplace. "My, what a fine fire," said the woodcutter. "I wish we had a nice sausage to roast over it."

Before the woodcutter realized what he had said, a big fat sausage came bouncing across the room!

"Oh, you foolish man!" cried his wife. "Look what you have done. You could have wished for diamonds and rubies or even for a pot of gold. Instead, you wished for a sausage!"

"I'm sorry," said the woodcutter. "I didn't mean to do that. I'll make a better wish next time."

But his wife would not keep quiet. "A sausage! A sausage!" she scolded. "How could you ever have wished for a sausage?"

The woodcutter put his hands over his ears. "Enough about the sausage!" he cried. "I wish the silly thing would stick on the end of your nose!"

The words were barely out of his mouth when the sausage flew up and landed on his wife's nose where it stuck as tight as could be! The poor woman burst into tears.

"Oh dear! Oh dear!" said the woodcutter as he tried to comfort his wife. "I was going to wish that I was a king and then you would have been my queen. But whoever heard of a queen with a sausage growing on the end of her nose? Now I will have to use my last wish to make the sausage disappear." And so he did.

The woodcutter never became a king, but he learned an important lesson. From that day on, he began enjoying all the good things he had instead of wishing for more. He stopped his grumbling, and he and his wife lived happily ever after.

Inter-Tribal Indian Ceremonial

An American Indian Celebration

INTER-TRIBAL INDIAN CEREMONIAL
An American Indian Celebration

A highlight of the year for Native American children in the Southwest is the four-day Inter-Tribal Indian Ceremonial, which begins on the second Thursday in August. Indian artists, dancers and rodeo cowboys from more than 50 tribes gather in the town of Gallup, New Mexico, to celebrate their traditions and cultures and to perform for visitors from around the world.

In the mornings the children can visit the Ceremonial Showroom where the finest work of Native American artists and craftspeople are displayed. They also can walk through the marketplace and watch weavers, potters, silversmiths and other artists at work making items for sale.

In the afternoons everyone gathers at the outdoor arena to watch the All-Indian Rodeo. Cowboys compete in events such as roping, steer wrestling and bronc and bull riding, hoping to win one of the coveted silver belt buckles that are awarded as prizes. Other events include Women's Barrel Racing and a Fruit Scramble for children from the audience, who get to keep whatever fruit they grab. Between events the children can snack on a variety of Native American foods such as fry bread, Pueblo chili stew, Navajo tacos and Zuñi meat pies.

Traditional Indian dances are also an important part of the Ceremonial. In the evenings the children can watch the Hoop, Deer, Buffalo and other dances performed by costumed dancers from many different tribes. They also look forward to seeing the dancers in the festive All-Indian Parade. On Saturday morning downtown Gallup fills with the sounds of drums and bells as dancers parade through the streets along with tribal bands playing traditional and contemporary music. Sometimes the children and their families dress in their native clothing and join the parade too.

Note: When planning your celebration, look for ways to introduce the Native American cultures of your own area. Help the children understand that there are many different Indian tribes, each with its own customs and traditions.

INDIAN CRAFTS

For your celebration set up areas in the room where the children can work on a variety of Indian crafts.

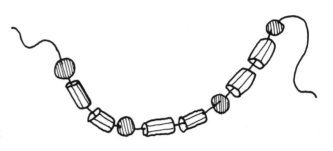

Necklaces — Let the children string beads made of playdough, colored straw sections and buttons on yarn. Encourage them to make patterns (a button, two straw sections, a bead, two straw sections, etc.).

Pots — Let the children shape pots out of balls of clay and etch designs on the sides with toothpicks. Or have them each start with a round flat base and build up the sides by coiling "snakes" of clay on top of one another.

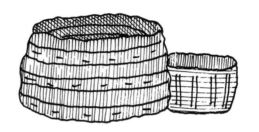

Weaving — Make a loom for each child by cutting five notches in both ends of a Styrofoam food tray and stringing yarn through the notches. Tape the yarn ends to the back of the tray. Then let the children use the over-under method to weave short strands of yarn, feathers and small sticks on their looms.

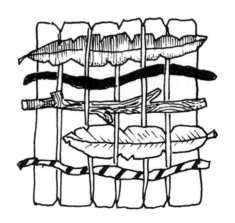

Variation: For younger children make looms by cutting slits all around the edges of Styrofoam trays and taping pieces of yarn to the backs. Then let the children wind the yarn around the trays, each time passing it through one of the slits.

Leatherwork — Let the children make "leather" by crumpling large shapes cut from brown grocery sacks and smoothing them out flat. Then let them use crayons or felt-tip markers to draw designs on their leather shapes.

SILVER BELT BUCKLES

At the All-Indian Rodeo, cowboys are awarded silver belt buckles as prizes. Let the children make their own buckles by gluing dried beans and macaroni on small ovals of cardboard. When the glue has dried, have them lay sheets of foil on top of their cardboard ovals and carefully press the foil around the glued-on items. Then have them fold the edges of the foil around the backs of the ovals. Punch holes at both ends of each oval and attach yarn pieces. Help the children tie their silver belt buckles around their waists after singing the rodeo song on p. 84.

INDIAN COUNTING GAME

Let the children play this version of an Indian counting game. Assemble five dried plum pits or cut five small circles out of cardboard. Paint a half-moon shape on one side of four of the pits and a star shape on one side of the remaining pit. Place the pits in a shallow basket or wooden bowl. Let one child at a time hold the basket and give it a shake. Then have the child count the number of shapes that turn up, alloting one point for each moon and two points for the star. The child who has the highest number of points at the end of the game wins.

MATCHING INDIAN DESIGNS

Draw matching Indian designs on six pairs of tongue depressors (check library books on Indian art for authentic design patterns). Then mix up the tongue depressors and let the children take turns finding the matching pairs.

Variation: Cut two parallel rows of six slits each in the bottom of a shoebox turned upside down. Then let the children insert matching pairs of tongue depressors in the slits.

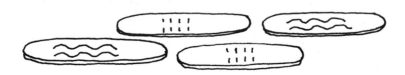

STORYTIME FUN

Read or tell the American Indian folktale "Mother Nature's Gift" on p. 87. Follow up with a discussion about rainbows. If it's a sunny day, take the children outside and try making a rainbow. Use a garden hose to spray a fine mist of water across the sun's rays. Then have the children stand with their backs to the sun and look for a rainbow in the mist.

MOVEMENT

ANIMAL DANCING

At the Ceremonial everyone enjoys watching traditional dances such as the Deer Dance and the Buffalo Dance. For your celebration let the children try dancing like different kinds of animals while you tap out rhythms on a hand drum. Talk about how different animals move (bears, rabbits, deer, turtles, etc.). Then adapt your drumbeats to fit each animal's movements.

CEREMONIAL PARADE

One of the highlights of the Ceremonial is the All-Indian Parade in downtown Gallup. Let the children celebrate by having a parade too. Provide them with drums, shakers and jingle bell bracelets to wear around their ankles. Then play library recordings of American Indian music (or use any appropriate music) and let the children march around the room.

AT THE RODEO

Sung to: "Mary Had a Little Lamb"

I will ride around the ring,
  (Trot around in a circle.)
Around the ring, around the ring.
I will ride around the ring
At the rodeo today.

I will ride a horse bareback,
  (Gallop around in a circle.)
A horse bareback, a horse bareback.
I will ride a horse bareback
At the rodeo today.

I will ride a bucking horse,
  (Leap and prance.)
A bucking horse, a bucking horse.
I will ride a bucking horse
At the rodeo today.

I will try to rope a steer,
  (Pretend to throw rope.)
Rope a steer, rope a steer.
I will try to rope a steer
At the rodeo today.

I will win a silver buckle,
  (Trot around in a circle.)
A silver buckle, a silver buckle.
I will win a silver buckle
At the rodeo today.

At the end of the song, help the children put on their
silver belt buckles (from the Art activity on p. 82). Then
let them enjoy their "Fruit Scramble" snacks (see p. 85).

Jean Warren

84

NATURE APPRECIATION WALK

In keeping with the spirit of your American Indian celebration, take the children on a nature appreciation walk. Before the walk, discuss how the Indians lived in harmony with nature, taking from it only what they needed to survive. Encourage the children to look for beautiful things in nature and to explore with their senses of touch, smell and hearing. Talk about the importance of nature's creatures and how we can help protect and care for their environment. If desired, bring along a trash bag for the children to fill with any litter they find along the way.

FRUIT SCRAMBLE

Part of the fun for the children at the All-Indian Rodeo is participating in the Fruit Scramble. For an adapted version, try this. Cover a coffee can with construction paper on which you have drawn geometric border designs. Cut a large hole in the plastic lid. Then place an assortment of raisins and dried fruit bits in the can. Have the children take turns reaching into the can through the hole in the lid and grabbing a handful of fruit. Let them keep and eat as many pieces as they can hold.

INDIAN FRY BREAD

Let the children help make Indian fry bread to snack on for your celebration. In a large bowl mix together 4 cups flour, 3 tablespoons baking powder, 2 tablespoons powdered milk and 2 teaspoons salt. Add 2 cups of warm water, one at a time, and knead to make a stiff dough. Add more flour if the dough is too sticky. Let the children roll the dough into about 20 balls and then flatten and stretch them out thin. Poke a hole in the middle of each piece, then fry in deep fat (375 degrees), two at a time, until golden brown. Serve warm, either plain or with honey.

MOTHER NATURE'S GIFT

An American Indian Folktale Adapted by Jean Warren

One day while Mother Nature was out working in her garden, she heard the sound of angry voices. It was two of her children, the sun and the rain, arguing about which one of them was most important.

"I am the most important!" shouted the sun. "Without me nothing would grow!"

"No, I am most important!" shouted the rain. "Without *me* nothing would grow!"

Back and forth they argued, each one sure that he was more important than the other.

At last Mother Nature grew tired of listening to them quarrel. To teach them a lesson, she sent the sun to one side of the world and the rain to the other side.

Soon there was peace and quiet again, and Mother Nature went back to her work. At first the sun and the rain didn't like being separated. But then they decided that this would be the perfect chance to prove which one of them was most important.

Day after day, the sun shone down on one side of the world while the rain poured down on the other. Before long the land on the sun's side was dry and bare, and on the rain's side there were terrible floods.

When the sun and the rain realized what they had done, they were sorry. They went back to Mother Nature and apologized. "We know now that neither of us is more important than the other," they said. "We need each other, and the world needs both of us to help the plants and animals grow."

Mother Nature was happy that the sun and the rain had learned their lesson. To celebrate, she decided to give the world a special gift.

Across the sky she painted an arc of beautiful colors – red, orange, yellow, green, blue and purple. "The world needs both my children, the sun and the rain," she said. "Whenever they decide to visit the world at the same time, this arc will appear in the sky. When the world sees the rainbow, it will know that my children are happy working together."

Mid-Autumn Festival

A Vietnamese Celebration

MID-AUTUMN FESTIVAL
A Vietnamese Celebration

The biggest holiday of the year for children in Vietnam is the Mid-Autumn Festival, which is also celebrated as Children's Day. The festival takes place at the time of the harvest moon, usually sometime in September.

On the day of the festival, the children help their mothers make moon cakes, the special treats enjoyed by everyone on this holiday. The round cakes are made of sticky rice and filled with nuts, raisins and other fruits. Often, local contests are held to see who can make the tastiest rice cakes.

In the evening the children walk up and down the streets carrying lighted paper lanterns. Some of the lanterns are round and white like the moon, while others are brightly colored and fashioned into shapes such as fish, dragons, rabbits and boats.

When the children hear the sounds of drums and cymbals, they know that it's time for the dragon parades. Large and small dragons made of paper and cloth are carried through the streets by dancers, who dip and sway as they weave back and forth. The children march along beside the dancers, sometimes testing their bravery by darting out at the dragons with their lanterns. When the parades are over, the dancers celebrate by setting off hundreds of noisy firecrackers.

Later in the evening the children and their families gather under the full moon for songfests. The lighted lanterns twinkle far into the night as everyone joins in singing favorite folksongs.

FESTIVAL LANTERNS

Vietnamese children make colored paper lanterns in various shapes for the Mid-Autumn Festival. To achieve a similar effect, let the children make pretend waxed paper lanterns. For each child cut two fish shapes, bird shapes, butterfly shapes, etc. (about 12 inches wide) out of waxed paper. Give the children small pieces of different colored tissue paper to glue on their shapes. When they have finished, staple the edges of each child's shapes together with a handful of lightly crumpled waxed paper scraps stuffed inside. Poke a hole through the top of each lantern and reinforce the holes with gummed reinforcement circles. Then thread long pieces of string through the holes and tie the lanterns to the ends of Popsicle stick handles.

Variation: To make a different kind of lantern, let each child draw designs on a 9- by 12-inch sheet of colored construction paper. Turn each paper over and fold it in half lengthwise. Cut slits along the fold (about 1 inch apart) up to ½ inch below the long open edges of the paper. Unfold the paper, roll it lengthwise into a tall lantern shape and staple the ends together. Then attach a 9-inch strip of construction paper to make a handle.

FINGERPAINTING MOONS

Let the children fingerpaint harvest moons for your Mid-Autumn Festival celebration. Whip Ivory Snow powder with water to make a soft fluffy mixture. Then let the children fingerpaint with the mixture on large paper plates or circles cut from white construction paper. When they have finished, let them sprinkle on small amounts of silver glitter, if desired.

Variation: Let the children fingerpaint with shaving cream and omit the glitter.

COUNTING MOON CAKES

Let the children make "moon cakes" out of playdough. (For traditional cake shapes have them cut thick rounds out of the playdough with cookie cutters; otherwise, let them roll the playdough into moon-shaped balls.) Use the moon cakes for various counting activities with the group. Or place fifteen of the cakes on a table along with five paper plates numbered from 1 to 5. Then let the children take turns placing the appropriate number of cakes on each plate.

==== **LANGUAGE** ====

STORYTIME FUN

Read or tell the Vietnamese folktale "The Orange in the Hole" on p. 97. For a follow-up activity let the children experiment with the floating idea described in the story. Place a small orange in the bottom of a deep container. Then let the children fill the container with water and watch what happens to the orange.

MOON BOOK

Make moon shapes by cutting 8-inch circles out of white construction paper. At group time talk with the children about the round shape of the moon. Ask them to name other things they know about or can see that are round (a ball, a clock, a plate, etc.). Then hold up a moon shape for each child and ask him or her to complete this sentence: "The moon reminds me of a _____." Use a felt-tip marker to sketch details on the shape according to the child's response (if the child says "a wheel," draw spokes; if the child says "a pizza," draw pepperoni circles, etc.). Let the children color their shapes with crayons. Then have them glue their shapes on sheets of light blue construction paper and add any other details they wish (a stick for a lollipop, a string for a balloon, etc.). At the bottom of each paper write the child's name and the name of the round object that he or she created ("an orange," "a penny," etc.). Then fasten the papers together to make a book. On the cover write "The Moon Reminds Me Of . . . ." and glue on one of the white moon shapes.

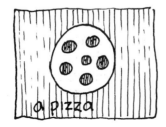
a pizza

a wheel

a lollipop

THE MOON

Use pictures from library books to discuss the different shapes (phases) of the moon. Call particular attention to the full moon and explain that it occurs about once a month. Encourage the children to tell about times when they have seen the full moon in the sky at night. What did the moon look like? How did the moonlight make the world around them look? In what ways is moonlight different from sunlight?

Extension: If desired, talk about how the Mid-Autumn Festival is held each year at the time of the harvest moon (the full moon that occurs closest to September 22-23). This moon was named "the harvest moon" because it shines so brightly that farmers were able to harvest their crops by its light.

DRAGON PARADE

Use a large paper grocery sack to make a dragon mask. Cut out eye holes and use felt-tip markers or paints to add facial features. Then let the children glue colored tissue paper or crepe paper strips all over the top and sides of the mask. When it's time for the parade, let one child at a time wear the dragon mask. Cover three or four other children with a piece of lightweight cloth and have them hook on behind the first child. Then use a drum and cymbals to beat out rhythms (or play appropriate music) and let the dragon wind and dance around the room while the rest of the children follow along behind carrying their paper lanterns from the Art activity on p. 91.

Extension: When the Dragon Parade is over, have a songfest and let the children sing their favorite songs. You might also want to include the two new songs on p. 94.

A GREAT BIG DRAGON

Sung to: "Little White Duck"

There's a great big dragon
Coming down our way,
A great big dragon,
On this holiday.
Let's grab our lanterns and follow along,
Dancing and waving as we sing our song.
There's a great big dragon
Coming down our way.
Hip, hip, hurray!

Jean Warren

FULL MOON

Sung to: "Row, Row, Row Your Boat"

Full moon shining bright,
   (Flutter fingers downward.)
Shining in the night.
What a lovely face you have,
   (Hold arms in circle above head.)
Big and round and white.

Susan A. Miller
Kutztown, PA

MOON CAKE SNACKS

Cut carrots, cucumbers and zucchini into rounds and let the children spread them with cream cheese.

Variation: Let the children spread cream cheese mixed with raisins and chopped nuts on round crackers.

MOON CAKE SANDWICHES

Let the children use a cookie cutter to cut rounds out of slices of white bread. Have them spread peanut butter on their rounds and gently press raisins into the peanut butter. Then let them sprinkle grated coconut all over the tops of their rounds. (To make fresh grated coconut, see recipe on p. 65.)

Variation: Instead of sprinkling on coconut, let each child place a second white bread round on top of the first one.

FRUIT BREAD MOON CAKES

Let the children help make banana bread or any other kind of bread that contains fruits and nuts. Bake the bread in well-greased soup or vegetable cans. Then slice the bread into rounds and let the children spread on cream cheese that has been mixed with a small amount of unsweetened frozen apple juice concentrate.

THE ORANGE IN THE HOLE

A Vietnamese Folktale Adapted by Jean Warren

Once upon a time some children were playing catch with an orange in a garden.

Everyone was having a good time until the orange accidentally dropped into a hole in the ground.

The children gathered around the hole, wondering what to do. Some tried to reach the orange with their hands, but the hole was too deep. Some tried to reach the orange with bamboo sticks, but that didn't work either.

At last, one clever child named Tu Anh had an idea. He went into a shed and got a large barrel, which he took to the well and filled with water. Then he carried the barrel over to the hole and poured the water inside it.

As quick as a wink, the orange bobbed to the top of the hole!

The children cheered when they saw the orange again, and they praised Tu Anh for his cleverness.

Then they picked up the orange and went happily back to playing their game of catch.

Diwali

An East Indian Celebration

DIWALI
An East Indian Celebration

The "brightest" holiday of the year for children in India is *Diwali,* or the Festival of Lights, which falls in late October or early November.

In the morning the children are eager to get up early. Their homes are spotless, since many days have been spent sweeping and scrubbing the rooms and whitewashing the walls. Garlands of flowers are hung in the doorways. And near the front entrances, good luck designs have been painted on the floor with colored rice flour.

Before getting dressed, the children take perfumed baths. Then they put on new clothes in honor of the holiday. Later in the morning the children help their mothers arrange little clay lamps around the house. The lamps have been purchased at bazaars and filled with oil. They are lined up along windowsills, doorways, paths and flat rooftops, each holding a tiny wick that will be lighted that night.

In the afternoon the children go with their families to visit relatives and friends, and at each house little boxes of sweets are exchanged. On the way home the children enjoy walking through the crowded bazaars where toys, candies, fruits and fireworks are for sale.

Then it's time for the true magic of Diwali. As night falls, thousands of tiny lamps and colored lights are lit, turning each village and town into a fairyland. The children hope that the twinkling lights will guide the goddess Lakshmi to their homes. A visit from Lakshmi on Diwali is sure to bring good luck and prosperity in the coming year.

DIWALI FLOOR DESIGNS

In preparation for Diwali, Indian families decorate their floors with colorful good luck designs made of wet or dry rice flour. Let the children celebrate the holiday by making their own good luck designs to place around the edges of the floor in your room. Fill plastic squeeze bottles with a runny mixture of flour and water. Set aside one bottle to use for white and add drops of red, yellow and blue food coloring separately to the other bottles. Then let the children squeeze the flour and water mixture on sheets of dark colored construction paper in any designs they wish.

Variation: Let the children draw their Diwali designs on construction paper with colored chalk. Or if it's a nice day, let them draw chalk designs on a sidewalk outside the room.

DIWALI LAMPS

Make a batch of playdough using your favorite recipe. Or mix together 1 cup flour, $\frac{1}{2}$ cup salt, 6 to 7 tablespoons water and 1 tablespoon vegetable oil. Add drops of food coloring, if desired. Let the children make little bowl-shaped lamps by flattening balls of playdough and pinching up the edges. Give them each a birthday candle (with the wick cut off) to place in the center of their lamps. Then line up the lamps on a windowsill to make a festive arrangement for your Diwali celebration.

Caution: The candles in the lamps are not to be lighted.

DIWALI FLANNELBOARD GAME

Cut five shallow bowl shapes out of brown felt to make Diwali lamps. Make lights for the lamps by cutting five flame shapes out of yellow felt. Use a black felt-tip marker to number the flame shapes from 1 to 5 and to draw corresponding numbers of dots on the lamp shapes. Place the lamp shapes on the flannelboard in random order. Then let the children take turns "lighting the Diwali lamps" by placing the numbered flame shapes above the appropriate bowl shapes on the flannelboard.

STORYTIME FUN

Read or tell the East Indian folktale "How Brave Bunny Tricked the Elephants" on p. 107. Talk with the children about the trick Brave Bunny played. Then let them pretend to be elephants taking their baths, rolling around in the water and splashing it over their backs with their long trunks.

Extension: Talk about how the moon used the lake as a mirror in the story. Place a large bowl of water on the floor under an overhead light so that the children can see its reflection. Then let them splash the water with their fingers and watch what happens.

SHADOW PUPPETS

Let the children make shadow puppets like those that are popular in India. Cut animal shapes (about 6 inches long) out of black construction paper. Have the children place their shapes on top of flat pieces of Styrofoam and punch designs in the shapes with toothpicks. When they have finished, attach Popsicle-stick handles to the shapes. Then set up a white sheet screen with a bright light behind it. Let the children experiment with moving their puppets between the light and the sheet to cast shadows. Encourage them to make up stories about animals and use their puppets to act out the movements.

Variation: Let the children play with their puppets while holding them up to a window so that the light shines through the punched designs.

Cathy Spagnoli
Seattle, WA

102

INDIAN SPICE BOOKS

If there's one word that describes Indian food, it's "spicy!" In some dishes just one spice is used, while in others there may be as many as fifteen. Let the children make spice books to use for sniffing and comparing some common spices used in Indian cooking. Set out small bowls of powdered spices such as cumin, coriander, turmeric, ginger, cinnamon and cloves. Give each of the children a small book made from construction paper. Then let them brush glue on their book pages and sprinkle pinches of the different spices on top of the glue.

FLOATING DIWALI LAMPS

On Diwali, girls in India sometimes light little lamps and float them in rivers or lakes. (Lamps that stay lit for a long time are thought to bring good luck.) For your celebration make floating Diwali lamps by cutting cups out of a Styrofoam egg carton. In the bottom of each cup, tape one end of a 2-inch piece of string to make a pretend wick. Attach a small piece of yellow tape to the top of the wick for a flame, if desired. Then fill a tub with water and let the children use the Diwali lamps as floating toys.

Caution: The wicks in the lamps are not to be lighted.

DANCING TO INDIAN MUSIC

Play library recordings of Indian music for the children to dance to. Give them jingle bell bracelets to wear around their ankles and divide them into two groups. Let one group sit on the floor and accompany the music with drums and other rhythm instruments while the other group dances. Then let the groups trade places.

103

PET THE ELEPHANT

Let small groups of children play this version of an Indian children's game. Choose one child to be the Elephant. Have the Elephant get down on all fours and begin swinging its trunk (one arm) back and forth and up and down. Then let the other children gather around and try petting the Elephant without getting touched by its swinging trunk. Whenever the Elephant's trunk touches someone, let that child be the new Elephant.

DIWALI NOW IS HERE
Sung to: "The Mulberry Bush"

Let's scrub-a-dub-dub the walls and floor,
   (Make scrubbing movements.)
Walls and floor, walls and floor.
Let's scrub-a-dub-dub the walls and floor,
Diwali *(dee-wah-lee)* now is here.

Let's take a bath and get all clean,
   (Make bathing movements.)
Get all clean, get all clean.
Let's take a bath and get all clean,
Diwali now is here.

Let's all put on our brand new clothes,
   (Make dressing movements.)
Brand new clothes, brand new clothes.
Let's all put on our brand new clothes,
Diwali now is here.

Let's go and visit all our friends,
   (Skip and bow.)
All our friends, all our friends.
Let's go and visit all our friends,
Diwali now is here.

Let's light our lamps and watch them glow,
   (Pretend to light lamps.)
Watch them glow, watch them glow.
Let's light our lamps and watch them glow,
Diwali now is here.

Let's all join hands and circle round,
   (Hold hands and walk in a circle.)
Circle round, circle round.
Let's all join hands and circle round,
Diwali now is here.

Elizabeth McKinnon

CHAPATIS

For your Diwali celebration let the children help make *chapatis* (Indian bread). Over a large bowl sift together 1 cup fine whole-wheat flour, 1 cup white flour and ½ teaspoon salt. If desired, stir in 1 tablespoon vegetable oil. Add ¾ cup lukewarm water and knead the dough for several minutes until smooth and elastic. Let stand, covered, for 30 minutes. Shape the dough into 8 balls and roll them out into 6-inch circles on a floured surface. To cook each chapati, place a frying pan over medium heat and brush with ½ teaspoon oil. Fry the chapati for 1 minute, then brush oil over the top, turn it and fry for another minute or until brown spots and bubbles appear. When the chapatis are done, cut them into wedges and spread with butter or Peanut Chutney (see recipe below). Makes 8 chapatis.

Cathy Spagnoli
Seattle, WA

PEANUT CHUTNEY

Let the children help shell peanuts (leaving on the brown skins) to fill 1 cup. In a blender container combine ½ cup water, 2 cloves garlic, the juice of ½ lime or lemon, a pinch of red pepper (optional) and salt to taste. Blend for 1 minute. Then add peanuts (and a touch more water, if necessary) and continue blending to a coarse consistency. To serve, spread on chapatis or slices of bread.

Cathy Spagnoli
Seattle, WA

HOW BRAVE BUNNY TRICKED THE ELEPHANTS

An East Indian Folktale Adapted by Elizabeth McKinnon

Long ago Brave Bunny and his rabbit friends were playing in the grass beside a lake.

Suddenly one of the rabbits pricked up her ears. "I hear a noise," she said.

"It sounds like thunder," said another rabbit.

But it wasn't thunder. It was a herd of thirsty elephants stomping through the forest. They were looking for a place to get a cool drink.

When the elephants reached the edge of the water, the rabbits hopped to the top of a hill. "Those elephants are taking over our lake," they said. "If we try to play there again, we'll get stepped on. What shall we do?"

"Don't worry," said Brave Bunny. "I know how to make those elephants go away. Just wait until tonight and I will show you."

That evening when the moon was shining in the sky, the elephants began taking their baths. The huge animals rolled about in the lake, splashing water everywhere with their long trunks.

From the hilltop Brave Bunny called, "Hello, Elephants! I have a message for you from the moon. She wants you to know that she is angry with you. This lake is her mirror. She looks into it every night when she combs her white hair. But now you are splashing around in the water, and she can't see her face. She says you must go away at once or else she will punish you!"

The elephants stopped their splashing. They knew that the moon was very powerful, and they were afraid. "What will she do to punish us?" they asked.

"She will stop shining in the sky," said Brave Bunny. "Then it will be so dark you won't be able to see at all. You don't want that to happen, do you?"

"No, no!" cried the elephants. "Please tell the moon we will go away right now. And we promise that we'll never come back."

When the elephants went off into the forest, the rabbits said, "That was a good trick you played, Brave Bunny. Even though you are small, you were able to get rid of those big elephants by using your head."

Then the rabbits hopped back down the hill to the grassy shores of their lake where they played happily and in peace from that time on.

Hanukkah

A Jewish Celebration

HANUKKAH
A Jewish Celebration

Winter is a special time for Jewish children, for that is when they celebrate *Hanukkah,* or the Feast of Lights. The eight-day celebration, which begins in late November or December, commemorates the rededication of the Temple of Jerusalem more than 2,000 years ago. When it was time to light the sacred Temple lamp, only enough oil to keep it burning for one day could be found. But miraculously the lamp continued to burn for eight full days.

On *every* night of Hanukkah, the children gather with their family around the Hanukkah *menorah,* a special candelabrum that holds nine candles. First a parent lights the *shammash* (server candle), which usually stands a little higher than the others in the center of the menorah. After traditional blessings are recited, the shammash is used to light one candle on the first night, two candles on the second night and so on, until the last night when all eight candles are lit.

After the lighting of the menorah, the children usually receive presents, one on each night of the Hanukkah celebration. A favorite gift for young children is a *dreidel,* a cube-shaped top that has the Hebrew letters *nun*, *gimel*, *hay* and *shin* written on its sides. These letters stand for words that mean "a great miracle happened there," referring to the oil that lasted for eight days in the Temple of Jerusalem. The children love spinning their dreidels and using them to play traditional games.

Hanukkah is also the time for enjoying cheese or potato *latkes,* crisp fried pancakes that are served with applesauce and sour cream. The children learn that eating foods cooked in oil is another way of remembering the miracle of the lamp that burned for eight days in the holy Temple.

HANUKKAH MENORAHS

Let the children make menorahs for your Hanukkah celebration. For bases cut 12- by 2-inch strips out of heavy cardboard and paint them dark blue or cover them with dark blue construction paper. Give the children large lumps of playdough and sprinkle gold glitter on a tabletop. Let the children work the glitter into the dough. Then have them each use their playdough to make eight 1-inch balls and one 2-inch ball. Show them how to line up the nine balls on their cardboard bases with the largest ball in the

center. When they have finished, give them each nine white birthday candles (with the wicks cut off) to stand upright in their menorahs.

Caution: The candles in the menorahs are not to be lighted.

PAINTING WITH DREIDELS

Make a "dreidel" for each child by cutting a 2-inch square out of a file folder. Using a ruler, draw two diagonal lines across the square from corner to corner and write the Hebrew letters *nun, gimel, hay* and *shin* in the four sections (see illustration). Use a large needle to poke a hole in the center of the square where the lines intersect. Remove the cotton from one end of a Q-Tip and insert the Q-Tip halfway through the hole. Adjust the square so that it is perpendicular to the Q-Tip and squeeze drops of glue around

the hole to hold the square in place. When the glue has dried, set out the dreidels along with sheets of white construction paper and shallow containers of blue tempera paint. Let the children practice spinning their dreidels with their fingers on a flat surface. Then let them dip the cotton ends of their dreidels into the paint and spin them on their papers to create swirling designs.

Variation: Set out more than one color of paint and make dreidels to use for each separate color.

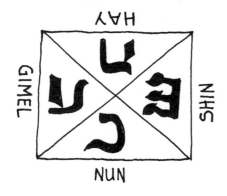

DREIDEL SPINNING GAME

Let the children try this version of the traditional Hanukkah dreidel game. Make a dreidel by following the directions given in the activity "Painting With Dreidels" on p. 111. Label the four sections on the dreidel "0," "All," "½" and "1." Have the children sit on the floor in a circle and give each child ten dried beans. Have everyone put one or two beans into the pot (a bowl placed in the center of the circle). Then let one child begin by spinning the dreidel. If it lands on "0," the child gets nothing; if it lands on "All," the child gets the whole pot; if it lands on "½," the child gets half the pot; if it lands on "1," the child must add one bean to the pot. Continue playing, having everyone put one or two beans into the pot before each child's turn. The player who ends up with the highest number of beans at the end of the game wins.

STAR OF DAVID NUMBER GAME

Make a Star of David number matching game for the children to play at Hanukkah time. To make ten stars, cut twenty 4-inch triangles out of heavy paper or tagboard. Make each six-pointed star by placing one triangle point up and gluing another triangle point down on top of it. Use a felt-tip marker to number five of the stars from 1 to 5 and to draw corresponding numbers of dots on the other five stars. Then mix up the stars and let the children take turns finding the matching pairs.

Valerie Bielsker
Lenexa, KS

STORYTIME FUN

Read or tell the Jewish folktale "The Two Brothers" on p. 117. Then talk with the children about the spirit of giving and why we give gifts to people we love at holiday time. How does it feel to receive presents? How does it feel when we give gifts to others?

Extension: If desired, follow up by letting the children make holiday gifts to take home (decorated bookmarks, illustrated note cards, etc.).

HANUKKAH CANDLES

For this flannelboard game cut a nine-holed Hanukkah menorah shape out of brown felt, nine candle shapes out of white or blue felt and nine candle flame shapes out of yellow felt. Place the menorah with the nine candles standing in it on the flannelboard. Put a flame shape on top of the middle candle. Explain that with a real menorah the candle in the center (the shammash) would be used to light the other candles. Then let the children take turns placing flame shapes on the eight remaining candles as you read the poem below. Remove all the flames after each verse so that the next child can "light" the appropriate number of candles.

Variation: If desired, leave the menorah on the flannelboard throughout Hanukkah and let the children "light" the appropriate number of candles each day.

Eight little candles in a row,
Waiting to join the holiday glow.

The first night we light candle number one.
Hanukkah time has now begun.

The second night we light candles one and two.
Hanukkah's here — there's lots to do.

The third night we light all up to three.
Hanukkah's here — there's lots to see.

The fourth night we light all up to four,
Each now a part of the Hanukkah lore.

The fifth night we light all up to five,
Helping our Hanukkah come alive.

The sixth night we light all up to six.
Happy candles — happy wicks.

The seventh night we light all up to seven.
The glow of each candle reaches to heaven.

The eighth night we light all up to eight.
Hanukkah's here — let's celebrate!

Jean Warren

CANDLE CLOCK

Try this candle activity during your Hanukkah celebration to help the children visualize the concept of time. Place two candles that are the same length in candle holders. Burn one candle for 30 minutes. Measure the difference in length between the two candles. Then use that measurement to mark lines down the side of the un-burned candle. Set the first candle aside and light the marked candle while the children watch.

Explain that when the candle burns down to the first line, 30 minutes will have gone by; when it burns down to the second line, another 30 minutes (or 60 minutes) will have gone by, etc. Then let the children periodically check the candle as it burns.

Caution: Activities that involve lighted candles require adult supervision at all times.

FIVE LITTLE DREIDELS

Cut five large dreidel shapes out of construction paper or tagboard. Then let the children take turns holding the shapes and acting out the movements as you recite the poem below.

Five little dreidels spinning in a row.
The first one spun, oh, so slow.
The second one went round and round.
The third one fell down on the ground.
The fourth one spun like a happy top.
The fifth one said, "I'll never stop!"
Five little dreidels — look and see,
Spinning at Hanukkah for you and me.

Marjorie Debowy
Stony Brook, NY

EIGHT LITTLE CANDLES

Sung to: "Twinkle, Twinkle, Little Star"

Eight little candles in a row,
Waiting to join the holiday glow.
We will light them one by one,
Until all eight have joined the fun.
Eight little candles burning bright,
Filling the world with holiday light.

Jean Warren

I'M A LITTLE DREIDEL

Sung to: "I'm a Little Teapot"

I'm a little dreidel *(dray-dul)*
Made of clay.
Spin me around
When you want to play.
When I fall down, if you don't win,
Just pick me up and spin again!

Adapted Traditional

===== **SNACKS** =====

CHEESE LATKES

Make cheese latkes for the children to enjoy at Hanukkah time. Use a blender to combine 3 eggs, ¼ cup milk, 1 cup cottage cheese and ¼ teaspoon salt. Add 1 cup flour and blend again. Spoon the batter into a hot greased frying pan to make 3-inch rounds. Fry on both sides until golden brown. Drain on paper towels, then serve warm with sour cream, yogurt or applesauce (see recipe below). Makes 18 latkes.

APPLESAUCE

Let the children help quarter, core and peel 3 to 4 sweet apples. Cut the quarter pieces in half and place them in a saucepan with ½ cup water. Sprinkle on ½ teaspoon cinnamon, then simmer for about 20 minutes or until tender. Let the children mash the cooked apples with a potato masher or whirl the apples in a blender. Serve with cheese latkes. Makes 6 small servings.

THE TWO BROTHERS

A Jewish Folktale Adapted by Jean Warren

Once upon a time there were two brothers. One brother had a wife and children. The other brother was not married.

The brothers were farmers. Between their two farms was a large hill.

One year both brothers had very good harvests. Each had more than he needed.

The first brother, who was married, decided to give part of his crop to his single brother so that his brother could stop working and look for a wife.

"I know what I will do," he said. "Tonight I will sneak over the hill and leave part of my crop in my brother's field."

Meanwhile, the single brother was looking over his abundant crop. He knew that he had much more than he needed.

"I think I will share my crop with my brother," he said. "He is married and needs more food than I do. I will sneak over the hill tonight and leave part of my crop in my brother's field."

When nighttime came, the brothers loaded up their extra crops in bags and carried them to the top of the hill.

When the brothers met at the top of the hill, they realized what had happened. Then they hugged each other and laughed because they loved each other so much.

And one day, a city was built on top of the hill where the brothers met. It became known as Jerusalem, the city of peace and love.

Christmas in Mexico

A Mexican Celebration

CHRISTMAS IN MEXICO
A Mexican Celebration

Christmas is truly a festive time for children in Mexico. Around the second week in December, they begin helping their families set up Nativity scenes. In the markets they visit stalls filled with brightly colored Christmas toys, lanterns, hand-carved figurines and flaming red poinsettias. For holiday snacks they stop at little street corner stands to buy candied nuts, fruits and other sweets.

But it is the night of December 16 the children look forward to, for that is the beginning of *Las Posadas.* On each of the nine nights before Christmas, the children and their families reenact the story of Mary and Joseph's search for a place to stay in Bethlehem. Holding lighted candles, they walk in a procession from house to house, singing a song in which they ask for lodging. At each house they are turned away until finally they reach the place where the evening's festivities are to be held. There they are welcomed and invited to come in for a party.

For the children, the highlight of the party is the breaking of the *piñata,* a clay pot shaped like a bird or an animal that is covered with bits of colored tissue paper and filled with candies, fruits, nuts and small toys. The piñata is hung from the ceiling by a rope. Then one at a time the children are blindfolded and given a stick with which they try to break the piñata while an adult pulls the rope up and down. When the piñata is finally broken and the goodies fall to the ground, the children scramble to pick them up.

On Christmas Day some children may get presents, but traditionally, they must wait until Three Kings Day on January 6. The night before, they leave out their shoes. Then the next morning they find their shoes filled with presents left by the Three Kings, who long ago brought gifts for the Baby Jesus.

FOIL CHRISTMAS ORNAMENTS

Many Christmas ornaments that come from Mexico are made out of brightly colored tin. To achieve a similar effect, let the children use foil cupcake liners and colored tissue paper to create ornaments. Pass out the foil liners and have the children smooth them flat with their hands. Let them tear various colors of tissue paper into ½-to 1-inch pieces. Then have them brush glue on their liners and lay the tissue paper pieces on top of the glue. Encourage them to leave a little foil showing around the edges of their liners and to overlap their tissue pieces. When the glue has dried, punch holes in the tops of the ornaments and tie on loops of yarn for hangers.

MEXICAN SERAPES

To get in the spirit of your Mexican celebration, let the children make *serapes* (Mexican blankets) to wear over their shoulders. For each child carefully tear off a four-piece section from a roll of heavy-duty white paper towels. On the back of each section tape over the perforated lines so that the towels will not come apart. Let the children snip fringes along the short ends of their towel sections (or cut the fringes yourself). Then let them use bright colors of fairly thick tempera paint to decorate their serapes with stripes, dots or other designs. When the paint has dried, let the children wear their serapes draped over one shoulder or wrapped around both shoulders and fastened in front with safety pins.

COUNTING CHRISTMAS TOYS

Give each child a large precut shoe shape to glue on a sheet of white construction paper. Talk about how Mexican children find their presents tucked inside their shoes on the morning of Three Kings Day. Choose a number you are working on and write it on each child's paper. Then let the children tear pictures out of toy catalogs and glue the corresponding number of "presents" on their shoe shapes.

Variation: Have the children sit on the floor and take off one of their shoes. Then place different numbers of small toys in the shoes for the children to count.

121

STORYTIME FUN

Read or tell the Mexican folktale "The Flower of Christmas Eve" on p. 127. Talk with the children about the true meaning of gift giving at Christmastime. Then display a colored picture of a poinsettia plant and help the children to see that the red petals are actually red leaves. Explain that the true flowers are the little yellow centers around which the red leaves grow.

Caution: If you prefer showing a real poinsettia, avoid letting the children touch it. Although poinsettias are not toxic, the sap can be irritating to the eyes and mouth.

GROWING AN AVOCADO PLANT

Pass around a large ripe avocado for the children to touch and examine. Then cut it open and let the children taste the meat (or save it for making the Snack recipe on p. 125). Remove the pit and stick three toothpicks horizontally into its sides near the pointed end. Then balance the toothpicks on the rim of a glass jar filled with water so that the rounded end of the pit is covered. After four to six weeks, watch for roots to begin to form. Soon a stem will emerge from the top of the seed, then leaves will appear. When the stem is about 12 inches tall, plant the avocado in a large pot and place it in bright sunlight.

Hint: If you want your plant to form branches, cut a few inches off the top of the stem when it's about 8 inches tall.

PIÑATA FUN

Making a Piñata — Let the children help decorate a large paper grocery bag to make a bird piñata. Glue construction paper eyes and a beak on one side of the bag. Partially fill the bag with treats (sticks of sugarless gum, unshelled peanuts, small boxes of raisins, balloons, etc.). Fill out the bag by adding lightly crumpled newspaper and tie it closed at the top with twine. Let the children glue short strips of different colored tissue paper or crepe paper all over the bird piñata for feathers. If desired, glue on construction paper wings, legs and a tail. Then hang the piñata from the ceiling.

Breaking the Piñata — Have the children circle around the piñata while singing the piñata song on p. 124. Then have them sit down on the floor in a wide circle. Stand in the center of the circle holding a plastic bat. Pretend to close your eyes and turn around several times. Then have the children give you directions for hitting the piñata. Each time you get ready to take a swing, ask a question such as: "Should I step forward or backward? Should I take one step or two steps? Should I swing higher or lower? Should I swing to the left or to the right?" When you finally break the piñata, let the children scramble to pick up the treats.

Hint: Establish rules for sharing the treats before breaking the piñata and have extra treats on hand in case they are needed.

Variation: Let the children use paper lunch bags to make individual piñatas and place a few selected treats in each bag before tying them closed.

MEXICAN HAT DANCE

Place a *sombrero* (Mexican hat) or any kind of large hat on the floor and let the children dance around it as they sing the song below. For a festive touch let them wear sashes made of colored crepe paper streamers around their waists.

Sung to: "La Raspa"
(Mexican Hat Dance Song)

Let's dance and dance and dance,
Around the hat let's dance.
Let's dance and dance and dance,
Around the hat let's dance.
Tra-la-la-la-la-la-la-la-la-la,
Tra-la-la-la-la-la-la-la-la-la.
Tra-la-la-la-la-la-la-la-la-la,
Around the hat let's dance.

Jean Warren

DANCING WITH MARACAS

Make festive *maracas* (shakers) to use for your Mexican celebration. To make each maraca, put dried beans or rice into a paper cup. Place another paper cup upside down on top of the first cup and tape the rims together. Let the children decorate their maracas by gluing thin strips of colored tissue paper or crepe paper on the ends. When the glue has dried, play library recordings of Mexican songs (or use any appropriate music) and let the children dance while shaking their maracas.

Variation: Make maracas by stapling paper plates together and placing beans or rice inside. Cover the staples with tape before the children add decorations.

====== MUSIC ======

FELIZ NAVIDAD

Sung to: "The Farmer in the Dell"

Feliz Navidad *(fey-lees nah-vee-dahd)*,
Feliz Navidad.
Merry Christmas everyone,
Feliz Navidad.

Explain to the children that *Feliz Navidad* means "Merry Christmas" in Spanish.

Jean Warren

HERE IS OUR PIÑATA

Sung to: "Sing a Song of Sixpence"

Here is our piñata *(pee-nya-tah)*,
What a sight to see,
Filled with treats and goodies
Just for you and me.
When it's time to break it,
We will circle round.
Then we'll scramble for the treats
That fall down to the ground.

Elizabeth McKinnon

124

CHEESE NACHOS

Turn snack time into *fiesta* time by using brightly colored construction paper for placemats and arranging paper or artificial flowers in the center of the table. Let the children help make cheese *nachos* (appetizers) by breaking hard *taco* shells into bite-sized pieces and sprinkling them with grated cheese. Then place the chips on a cookie sheet and bake at 350 degrees until the cheese has melted.

Variation: To make your own corn chips, combine ½ cup yellow cornmeal and ½ teaspoon salt in a mixing bowl. Pour in 1 cup boiling water and stir. Add 1 teaspoon margarine and stir until melted. Add another ¾ cup boiling water and continue stirring. Drop small spoonfuls of the mixture (about the size of a half-dollar) on a greased cookie sheet. Then bake at 425 degrees for 12 to 15 minutes or until lightly browned. Makes approximately 3 dozen chips.

GUACAMOLE

Let the children help make *guacamole* (avocado dip) to eat with plain taco chips or corn chips. Peel a large ripe avocado and remove the pit. Mash the avocado with a fork in a small bowl.

Add ½ cup chopped tomato, ½ teaspoon minced onion and 1 tablespoon fresh lemon juice. Stir well, then serve in small cups or on top of lettuce leaves.

126

THE FLOWER OF CHRISTMAS EVE

A Mexican Folktale Adapted by Jean Warren

Long ago in a small Mexican village there lived a girl named Maria and her little brother Pablo. Maria and Pablo were very poor, but they always looked forward to the Christmas festival. Each year a large Manger scene was set up in the village church, and the days before Christmas were filled with processions and parties.

Maria and Pablo loved Christmas. But one thing made them sad. Because they were so poor, they had no money to buy presents. They especially wished that they could give something to the church for the Baby Jesus. But they had nothing.

On Christmas Eve, Maria and Pablo set out for church to attend the Christmas service. Along the way they saw some bright green plants growing by the roadside.

"I know," said Maria. "Let's take these plants with us to give to the Baby Jesus."

"All right," said Pablo.

So the children gathered up the plants and took them to the church where they placed them around the Manger. Some of the other children teased them because they had no better presents to offer. But Maria and Pablo said nothing. They knew they had given what they could.

Then during the church service a wonderful thing happened. All around the Manger the plants that Maria and Pablo had brought began to change color. One by one the green leaves on top of the plants turned into bright red petals, and soon the Manger was surrounded by beautiful starlike flowers.

From that time on, people in Mexico began calling the green plant with the bright red petals "The Flower of Christmas Eve." Others came to call it the poinsettia, and to this day it is a favorite flower at Christmastime everywhere.

Christmas in Germany

A German Celebration

CHRISTMAS IN GERMANY
A German Celebration

Children in Germany begin looking forward to Christmas around the end of November. They receive Advent calendars to use for counting the number of days until Christmas. And in each home they help make an Advent wreath that holds four red candles, one for lighting on each of the four Sundays before Christmas.

On the night of December 5, the children wait for a visit from Saint Nicholas, a tall bearded man who wears a bishop's robe and hat. Saint Nicholas makes his rounds riding on a white horse and carrying a bag filled with cookies, fruits and nuts. Sometimes the children fill their shoes with hay and leave them out with a bowl of water for Saint Nicholas' horse. Then in the morning they find small toys and other treats inside their shoes.

Between December 6 and Christmas the children visit fairs where booths are piled high with toys, candies, gingerbread cookies, Christmas trees and brightly colored ornaments. When they get hungry, they stop for snacks of hot sausages or plump salty pretzels.

On Christmas Eve the children in each family wait outside the Christmas room while their parents make final preparations. Then they go inside where they see the decorated Christmas tree for the first time. Around the tree, stacked on little tables, are gaily wrapped presents that have been left by the Christ Child. Before the children open their presents, they join hands with their parents and sing *"O Tannenbaum"* ("O Christmas Tree").

Many well-loved Christmas customs come from Germany, including the tradition of the Christmas tree. One story says that on a starry Christmas Eve, Martin Luther was so moved by the beauty of a snow-covered fir tree that he cut it down and took it home for his children. Then he decorated the tree with lighted candles to represent stars.

ADVENT CALENDAR

Let the children make a paper chain Advent calendar to use for counting the number of days until Christmas. Have them glue colored construction paper strips together to make a chain of 24 loops. Then let them tear small pictures of toys from Christmas catalogs and glue one picture on each loop. Hang up the calendar on December 1. Then each day remove one loop and let the children count how many are left.

Variation: Let the children decorate the calendar with Christmas stickers instead of pictures torn from catalogs.

GLITTER ENVELOPES

In some places in Germany, children write letters to the Christ Child to tell Him what they want for Christmas. To make sure that He sees their letters, they glue sugar on the envelopes for sparkle and place them on a windowsill before going to bed. For your celebration let the children draw pictures of what they want from Santa and place the pictures in envelopes. Then let them brush glue on their envelopes and sprinkle on sugar or glitter for catching Santa's eye.

Variation: Instead of drawing pictures, let the children tear pictures out of Christmas catalogs and glue them on sheets of paper.

ADVENT WREATHS

Give each of the children a small plastic lid with a hole cut out of the center. Let them make wreaths by rolling green playdough into "snakes" and pressing the playdough into their plastic lids. Then give them each four red birthday candles (with the wicks cut off) to stand upright in their wreaths.

Variation: Use uncolored playdough and let the children decorate the tops of their wreaths with evergreen sprigs.

Caution: The candles on the wreaths are not to be lighted.

A VISIT FROM SAINT NICHOLAS

Have the children sit on the floor in a circle. Place five or six toys in the center of the circle for them to see. Then place the toys in a box. Choose one child to be Saint Nicholas. While the other children close their eyes, have Saint Nicholas put one of the toys from the box inside a pillowcase. When the other children open their eyes, have Saint Nicholas walk around the circle and let each child try to guess which toy is inside the pillowcase by feeling it. Let the first child to guess correctly be the new Saint Nicholas.

MATCHING GINGERBREAD COOKIES

Cut six pairs of different cookie shapes out of brown paper or cardboard (trace around Christmas cookie cutters to make patterns). Use a black felt-tip marker to draw matching designs on each pair, if desired. Decorate a coffee can to make a "cookie jar" and place the cookie shapes inside it. Then let the children take turns emptying the cookie jar and finding the matching pairs of cookies.

EVERGREENS

Discuss how evergreen trees, wreaths and branches are used for Christmas decorations in Germany and other countries. Then take the children on a nature walk to collect branch tips from various kinds of evergreens. Along the way, point out the difference between evergreens and other trees and shrubs that have shed their leaves for the winter. When you get back to the room, talk about the color, smell and texture of the different evergreens you collected.

Variation: Plan a field trip to a Christmas tree lot to see the various kinds of evergreen trees on display. Make arrangements beforehand for obtaining branch tips to take back with you.

Extension: Cut Christmas tree or wreath shapes out of white or green construction paper. Then let the children paint on their shapes with evergreen branch tips dipped in green tempera paint.

FOUR LITTLE CANDLES

For this flannelboard game cut an Advent wreath shape out of green felt, four red candle shapes out of red felt and four candle flame shapes out of yellow felt. Place the wreath on the flannelboard and put the four candles upright on the wreath. Then read the poem below and let the children take turns placing the flames on the candles.

Variation: If desired, leave the wreath on the flannelboard throughout Advent and let the children "light" one of the candles each week.

Four little candles all in a ring,
Announcing the coming of our King.

The first week we light candle number one.
The Christmas season has now begun.

The second week we light candle number two.
Christmas is coming — there's lots to do.

The third week we light candle number three.
Set out the manger for all to see.

The fourth week we light candle number four.
The Christ Child is coming — let's Him adore.

Jean Warren

STORYTIME FUN

Read or tell the German folktale "The Spiders' Surprise" on p. 137. Follow up by letting the children pretend to be spiders dancing in the Christmas tree branches and leaving them covered with cobwebs.

Extension: Make cone-shaped Christmas trees out of green construction paper. Then let the children decorate their trees by gluing on strands of tinsel.

OUR CHRISTMAS TREE

Talk about how the tradition of the Christmas tree came from Germany. Then recite the poem below and let the children act out the movements.

We went out looking for a Christmas tree.
(Cup hand over eye and start walking.)
We went to see what we could see.
(Look all around.)
The first tree we found was much too small.
(Lower hands down near floor.)
The second tree we found was much too tall.
(Raise hands up high.)
The third tree we found was much too broad.
(Spread arms out wide.)
The fourth tree we found was thin as a rod.
(Hold up one arm.)

The fifth tree we found looked just about right.
(Make outline of tree with hands.)
So we chopped it down with all our might.
(Pretend to chop down tree.)
We took our tree home and set it straight.
(Pretend to set up tree.)
Everyone thought that it looked just great.
(Clasp hands and smile.)
Then we all joined hands and circled round
(Hold hands and move in a circle.)
The beautiful tree that we had found.

Jean Warren

PUMPERNICKEL TREATS

Gingerbread cookies are a traditional German favorite at Christmastime. For a sugarless alternative use cookie cutters to cut Christmas shapes out of slices of pumpernickel bread. Make "frosting" by adding drops of food coloring to whipped cream cheese. Then let the children spread the cheese on their pumpernickel shapes and add raisins, nuts and dried fruit bits for decorations.

GIANT PRETZELS

Let the children help make pretzels for your German Christmas celebration. Dissolve 1 package yeast in $1\frac{1}{2}$ cups warm water (105 to 115 degrees) and add $\frac{1}{2}$ teaspoon sugar. Stir in $4\frac{1}{2}$ cups flour and knead for 6 minutes. Let the dough rise, covered, in a greased bowl until double in size. Then divide the dough into 12 pieces and let the children roll them into long sticks. Blend together 1 egg yolk and 2 tablespoons water and have the children brush small amounts of the mixture on their pretzel sticks. Then let them sprinkle on some coarse salt or sesame seeds. Help the children lay their pretzel sticks on a cookie sheet in any shapes they wish. Then bake for 12 minutes at 450 degrees. If desired, keep the pretzels warm in a crock pot set on low. Makes 12 giant pretzels.

O TANNENBAUM
Sung to: "O Christmas Tree"

O Tannenbaum, O Tannenbaum,
(o tahn-en-baum, o tahn-en-baum)
Wie treu sind deine Blätter.
(vee troy zint die-nah blet-ter)
O Tannenbaum, O Tannenbaum,
(o tahn-en-baum, o tahn-en-baum)
Wie treu sind deine Blätter.
(vee troy zint die-nah blet-ter)
Du grünst nicht nur zur Sommerszeit,
(doo groonst nickt noor tsoor zohm-ers-tsite)
Nein, auch im Winter, wenn es schneit.
(nine, owk im vin-ter, venn es shnite)
O Tannenbaum, O Tannenbaum,
(o tahn-en-baum, o tahn-en-baum)
Wie treu sind deine Blätter.
(vee troy zint die-nah blet-ter)

O Christmas Tree, O Christmas Tree,
How lovely are your branches.
O Christmas Tree, O Christmas Tree,
How lovely are your branches.
Not only green in summertime,
But also green in wintertime.
O Christmas Tree, O Christmas Tree
How lovely are your branches.

Traditional

ADVENT SONG
Sung to: "Twinkle, Twinkle, Little Star"

Advent is a time to wait,
Not quite time to celebrate.
Light the candles one by one,
Till this Advent time is done.
Christmas Day will soon be here,
Time for joy and time for cheer!

**Karen Leslie
Erie, PA**

135

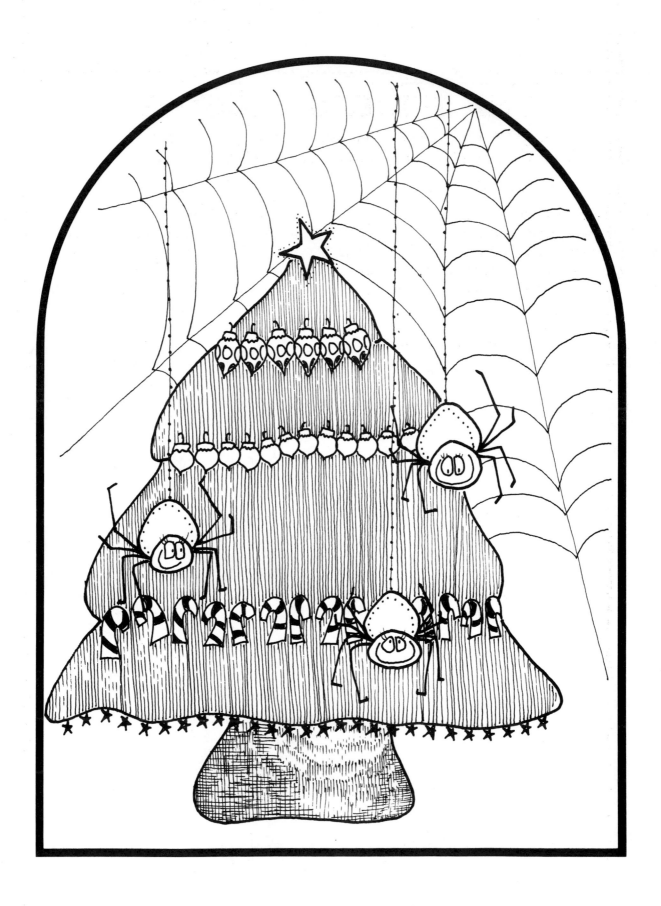

THE SPIDERS' SURPRISE

A German Folktale Adapted by Jean Warren

Long ago in Germany, families allowed their animals to come inside and view the Christmas trees on Christmas Eve. Because the Christ Child was born in a stable, they felt that the animals should be part of the Christmas celebration.

But the housewives never let the spiders come inside because they didn't want cobwebs all over their homes.

The spiders were very unhappy about this, so one year they complained to the Christ Child.

The Christ Child felt sorry for the spiders. Late that night He let them into the houses to see the Christmas trees.

The spiders loved the trees. All night long they danced in the branches, leaving them covered with cobwebs.

In the morning the housewives saw what the spiders had done. But instead of being angry, they were thrilled. For in the night the Christ Child had turned all the cobwebs into sparkling silver tinsel!

Kwanzaa

An African-American Celebration

KWANZAA
An African-American Celebration

For many African-American children, the last week in December is a very special time. Starting on December 26, the children and their families celebrate *Kwanzaa*, a seven-day festival that originated in the United States in the 1960s.

Kwanzaa means "first" in Swahili. The festival's customs and symbols come from African harvest celebrations of the first fruits of the year. It is a time for children and adults to commemorate their African heritage and to celebrate the values of family and community life.

Getting ready for Kwanzaa is part of the fun. In each home the children help make decorations of red, green and black (the colors of Kwanzaa) to hang on walls or an evergreen "Kwanzaa bush." A ceremonial table is set with a a straw mat, a candle holder for seven Kwanzaa colored candles, a unity cup and a bowl of fruits and vegetables. Every child in the family then places an ear of corn on the table.

On each night of Kwanzaa, the children gather with their parents to light one of the candles and to talk about one of the seven values of African-American family life: unity, self-determination, collective work and responsibility, cooperative economics, purpose, creativity and faith. Afterward, everyone drinks from the unity cup.

Throughout Kwanzaa the children often receive presents. In keeping with the spirit of the holiday, the presents usually include something homemade, a book and a heritage item such as African doll or art object. When the celebration ends on January 1, the children get together with their families and friends for joyous feasts that include African foods, music, dancing and singing.

KWANZAA DECORATIONS

Use a small Christmas tree to make a "Kwanzaa bush" for your celebration. Let the children decorate the bush with chains made from strips of red, green and black construction paper. Or cut geometric shapes out of black construction paper and let the children glue on small pieces of red and green giftwrap to make ornaments for hanging. If desired, let them sprinkle glitter on their ornaments while the glue is still wet.

Variation: Instead of using a real tree, cut a large Christmas tree shape out of green construction paper and mount it on a wall or a bulletin board. Then attach the children's decorations with tape or glue.

AFRICAN MASKS

Show pictures of African masks from library art books. Then let the children use paper plates to create African animal masks. Cut eye holes in the plates and cut nose and ear shapes out of construction paper (black for the zebra and leopard masks; gray for the elephant trunks and ears). Then let the children choose to make one or more of the following masks.

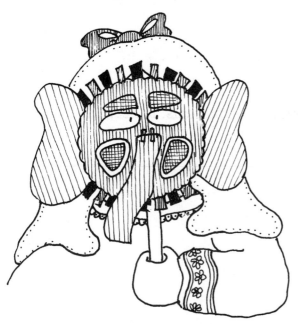

Zebra Masks — Paint the back sides of paper plates with vertical black stripes. When the paint has dried, glue on nose and ear shapes. Then glue short strips of tissue paper or crepe paper around the edges of the plates. (To keep the paint from smearing, glue ears and tissue paper strips to the unpainted sides of the masks.)

Leopard Masks — Paint the back sides of paper plates yellow. When the paint has dried, use black felt-tip markers or black paint to make spots. Glue on nose and ear shapes and add tissue paper strips.

Elephant Masks — Paint the back sides of paper plates gray. Glue on trunks, ears and tissue paper strips.

When the children have finished, display their masks on a wall or a bulletin board. Or attach tongue depressors for handles and let the children use them for dramatic play.

KWANZAA PLACEMATS

Let the children try this version of African cloth dyeing to make placemats for snack time. Have them dribble rubber cement in designs on sheets of white construction paper. Allow the glue to dry for about half an hour. Then have the children brush paint over the glue. When the paint has dried, let the children peel off the rubber cement to reveal the designs they created.

Variation: Have the children use white crayons to draw designs on white construction paper. Encourage them to press down hard while coloring. Then let them brush watery tempera paint over their designs.

Hint: If desired, cover the placemats with clear Con-Tact paper.

**Mary Haynes
Lansing, MI**

AFRICAN RING GAME

Here is a game that African children like to play in small groups. Provide the children with a sandbox and give one child a small plastic ring (or other small object). Let the other players make mounds in the sand. Then have them close their eyes while the child with the ring hides it in one of the mounds. When the other children open their eyes, have them search in the sand for the ring. Let the child who finds the ring first hide it the next time.

Variation: Use paper cups instead of sand and have the players try to guess under which cup the ring is hidden. Let the first child to guess correctly hide the ring for the next round.

SORTING KWANZAA COLORS

Set out three shoe boxes or coffee cans, one covered with red construction paper, one covered with green and one covered with black. Provide the children with an assortment of red, green and black items (buttons, small toys, crayons, yarn and fabric scraps, etc.). Then let them sort the items by placing them in the matching colored containers.

STORYTIME FUN

Read or tell the African folktale "How Spider Got His Thin Middle" on p. 147. Then show pictures of spiders so that the children can see how spider bodies are made up of two parts. Explain that one way to distinguish spiders from insects is to count their body parts: spiders have two parts, insects have three.

Extension: Talk with the children about harvest festivals and feasts. Draw a large rectangular mat shape on a piece of butcher paper. Then let the children tear pictures of foods out of magazines and seed catalogs and glue them on the mat to make a harvest feast mural.

KWANZAA CANDLES

For this flannelboard game cut a seven-holed candleholder out of brown felt. Cut out seven felt candle shapes, one black and three each of red and green. Then cut seven candle flame shapes out of yellow felt. Place the candleholder and candles on the flannelboard with the red and green candles alternating and the black candle in the middle. Then let the children take turns placing the flame shapes on the candles as you read the poem below.

Variation: If desired, leave the candleholder on the flannelboard throughout Kwanzaa and let the children "light" one of the candles each day.

Seven little candles all in a line,
Waiting to be lit at Kwanzaa time.

Who will light the black one?
(Child's name) will light the black one.

Who will light a red one?
(Child's name) will light a red one.

Who will light a green one?
(Child's name) will light a green one.
    (Continue until all candles are lit.)
Seven little candles all in a line,
Burning so bright at Kwanzaa time.

Now let's count them — one, two, three,
Four, five, six, seven candles to see!

Elizabeth McKinnon

143

HOW PEANUTS GROW

Set out unshelled peanuts for the children to crack open, examine and taste. Explain that peanuts are grown in many parts of Africa where they are called "groundnuts." Although we think of peanuts as nuts, they really belong to the same family as peas and beans. They grow underground on long shoots that the flowers on the peanut plants send down into the soil. Discuss how peanut shells contain from one to three nuts and how each nut is covered with a brown skin and divided into two parts. (When a raw peanut is planted, the sprout grows between the two halves.) If desired, let the children sample raw peanuts (available at health food stores) and compare the taste with that of roasted peanuts.

FUN WITH DRUMS

Set out a variety of objects for the children to use as drums. Oatmeal boxes and coffee cans with plastic lids can serve as hand drums. For larger drums place objects such as wastebaskets, ice-cream buckets and cardboard cartons upside down on the floor. Let the children experiment with the drums and talk about the different sounds they make. Which ones are best for making a sound like falling rain? Which ones are best for making the sound of elephants stomping? Tap out rhythms for the children to repeat. Then play library recordings of African music (or use Black American music) and let the children take turns accompanying the music with the drums while the others dance.

KWANZAA'S HERE
Sung to: "Three Blind Mice"

Red, green, black,
Red, green, black.
Kwanzaa's *(kwahn-zahs)* here,
Kwanzaa's here.
The decorations are quite a sight,
We light a candle every night,
The holiday is filled with light.
Kwanzaa's here.

Jean Warren

SWEET POTATO PIE

Let the children help make sweet potato pie for your Kwanzaa celebration. (Sweet potatoes are often used in African cooking.) To make the pie crust, mix together 1 cup white flour and ½ teaspoon salt. Cut in ⅓ cup shortening and add 3 tablespoons cold water. Knead and add a little more water, if necessary, until the dough can be formed into a ball. Roll out the dough on a floured piece of waxed paper. Then turn the paper upside down and ease the dough into a 9-inch pie pan. To make the pie filling, place the following ingredients into a blender container:

2 cups cooked sweet potatoes, 1 sliced banana, ¼ cup unsweetened frozen apple juice concentrate, ⅓ cup orange juice, 2 eggs and 1 teaspoon cinnamon. Blend well, then pour into the pie shell and bake at 400 degrees for 40 minutes. Makes 12 small servings.

Variation: Make sweet potato pudding by using just the pie filling ingredients above. Pour the blended mixture into a greased baking dish and bake at 350 degrees for 40 minutes. Serve warm or cold. Makes 8 to 10 small servings.

NUTTY BANANAS

Let the children enjoy this fun snack, which combines two favorite African foods — bananas and peanuts (groundnuts). Make a mixture of finely chopped or grated peanuts, wheat germ and cinnamon. Place small amounts of the mixture on paper plates and give each child one half of an unpeeled banana. To eat, have the children gradually peel their bananas and dip them into the nut mixture before taking each bite.

TASTY KWANZAA GIFTS

Giving homemade presents rather than store-bought ones is emphasized at Kwanzaa time. Let the children help make banana bread or any other kind of quick bread from a favorite recipe. Bake the bread in small metal juice cans to make individual loaves. Then let the children wrap the loaves and take them home as gifts.

Karen Seehusen
Ft. Dodge, IA

145

HOW SPIDER GOT HIS THIN MIDDLE

An African Folktale Adapted by Gayle Bittinger

Once upon a time Spider was big and fat and round. He was also very greedy. He lived in a forest near two villages. He liked living there because he was always sure of getting plenty of food to eat. If one village wasn't having a feast, the other village was.

But today was especially happy for spider. Both villages were having feasts. And Spider was so greedy that he planned to go to both of them.

"I don't want to miss anything good to eat," said Spider. "But how will I know which feast begins serving food first?"

Spider thought and thought until he came up with a plan. He got a long piece of rope and tied the middle of it around his fat body. Then he went and stood in the forest halfway between the two villages.

Soon a friend who was going to the feast at one village walked by. "Take this end of my rope and pull on it when the feast begins," Spider said.

Another friend came by on his way to the feast at the other village. "Take this other end of my rope and pull on it when the feast begins," said Spider.

Spider was very proud of himself for thinking of such a clever plan. Now all he had to do was wait for one of his friends to pull on the rope. Then he would know which feast was beginning first.

Spider thought about all the good food he would soon be eating. He thought about the yams and peppers. He thought about the meat cooking over the hot coals. Spider was getting very hungry.

Suddenly he felt a tug pulling him toward one village. Then he felt a tug pulling him toward the other village. The feasts had started at exactly the same time at both places. Both of Spider's friends were pulling on the ends of the rope. And the rope was getting tighter and tighter around his middle.

"Help!" shouted Spider. But no one heard him.

At the two villages the feasts went on for a long time. Spider's friends wondered why he did not come. They kept pulling and pulling on the ends of the rope while everyone was eating.

When the feasts were over, the friends went to find Spider. He was lying on the ground with the rope pulled tight around his middle. He looked very weak, and his middle looked very thin. His friends untied the rope. "Why didn't you come when the eating began?" they asked.

Spider was so weak he could barely whisper. "Because the two of you were pulling on the rope at the same time, and I couldn't move," he said. "The rope kept getting tighter and tighter. And now look at my middle. It's so thin."

Spider's middle never grew fat again. And to this day, if you look carefully, you can still see the thin middle that greedy Spider got on the day there were two feasts.

World Eskimo-Indian Olympics

An Alaskan Celebration

WORLD ESKIMO-INDIAN OLYMPICS
An Alaskan Celebration

A special treat for Native American children in Alaska is a visit to the World Eskimo-Indian Olympics, which are held each year in Fairbanks. Although the Olympics take place in late July, many of the same traditional games are played throughout the year at local celebrations and holiday get-togethers such as Christmas and New Year's.

All of the events that the children see reflect the rich cultural heritage of the Alaska Native Eskimo, Indian and Aleut people. There are arts and crafts displays and a Native Sewing Competition in which women make *mukluks* (boots), mittens and other traditional garments. There's a Parka Parade and an Indian Dress Contest. And when the Dance Teams perform, the children can see stories about animals and their importance to the Native people acted out onstage.

The athletic games are always fun to watch, too. In the Eskimo Blanket Toss, players are tossed high into the air by a team of "pullers" holding a big sealskin blanket. (This sport is similar to trampoline jumping.) In the Greased Pole Walk, players see how far they can walk or slide along a pole covered with grease. Other highlights include the Arm Pull, the Kneel Jump and the Knuckle Hop, which are all games that test strength and endurance. In the Four Man Carry, players use the same skills needed to pack game over long distances after a successful hunt.

Among other events the children can see are the Fish Cutting Competition and the Seal Skinning Contest. And everyone can take part in the Muktuk Eating Competition. *Muktuk,* the skin and top layer of meat from the bowhead whale, is a great delicacy that is enjoyed by children and adults alike.

Note: You may wish to supplement this celebration with your own ice and snow activities.

PAPER BAG MUKLUKS

Let the children make mukluks to wear for your Alaskan celebration. Give them each two brown paper lunch bags and have them decorate the sides with crayon designs. Then let them glue stretched-out cotton balls around the tops of their bags for a fur trim. To wear, have the children slip the bags over their feet. Then secure by tying thick yarn or twine around the tops of the bags.

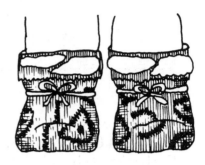

LACED MITTENS

For each child cut two mitten shapes out of brown poster board and punch holes around the edges. Let the children lace strands of colored yarn (taped at one end to make a "needle") through the holes. When they have finished, knot and trim the loose yarn ends on each mitten shape. Then tie each child's pair of mittens to-gether with a long piece of yarn so that the mittens can be worn over the child's shoulders.

Variation: If desired, let the children decorate their laced mittens with small pieces of cotton "fur."

WHALE TOOTH NECKLACES

Let the children try this version of Eskimo engraving to make "whale tooth necklaces." Cut whale tooth shapes (about $3\frac{1}{2}$ inches long) out of white Styrofoam food trays and let the children etch designs on them with toothpicks. To make the designs stand out, have the children brush black tempera paint over their shapes and then wipe them with damp paper towels. When the shapes have dried, punch holes in the tops and tie on loops of yarn to make necklaces.

ICE FISHING

Cut small fish shapes out of three different colors of construction paper. Place the shapes in a shoebox with a large hole cut in the lid. Have the children pretend that they are fishing through an ice hole in the Far North. Let them take turns reaching through the hole to "catch" the fish. Then have them sort the fish into three piles according to color.

LANGUAGE

STORYTIME FUN

Read or tell the Eskimo folktale "Why Mr. Fox Has a Red Coat" on p. 157. When the children have become familiar with the story, let them take turns acting out the roles of Mrs. Mouse and Mr. Fox.

Extension: Give each child a large fox shape cut out of white construction paper. Spray on puffs of shaving cream and let the children fingerpaint with it on their shapes. Then sprinkle on powdered red tempera paint and let the children continue fingerpainting to show how Mr. Fox's coat turned bright red.

SCIENCE

LAND OF THE MIDNIGHT SUN

Talk with the children about how days grow longer in summer and shorter in winter. Explain that in the arctic regions of Alaska the sun shines through much of the night in summertime and never rises at all for a few days in wintertime. Discuss what it might be like to have sunshine all night long. Would it be hard to go to sleep? How would it feel to be at school when it's dark all day?

152

ESKIMO-INDIAN OLYMPICS

Plan to hold your own "Olympics" and let the children play the non-competitive games below. Use the "pretend" suggestions to help the children understand how the games originated. When your Olympics are over, give everyone a "gold medal" sticker for being a winner.

Blanket Toss — Let two or more children hold the edges of a blanket and toss a stuffed animal into the air. (Pretend to be tossing a hunter high up so that he can spot game far away on the flat ice.)

Four Man Carry — Have each child walk from one side of the room to the other carrying as many stuffed animals as he or she can hold. (Pretend to be hunters packing game home across the ice after a successful hunt.)

Greased Pole Walk — Have the children walk heel-to-toe along a strip of masking tape attached to the floor. (Pretend to be fishermen walking across a river on a slippery log.)

Kneel-Jump — Have the children squat down and jump with both feet from one carpet square to another. (Pretend to be hunters jumping across floating pieces of ice.)

Arm Pull — Have two children sit on the floor facing each other with legs apart and feet touching. Then let them hold hands and pull back and forth. (Pretend to be hunters pulling game out of the water and across the ice.)

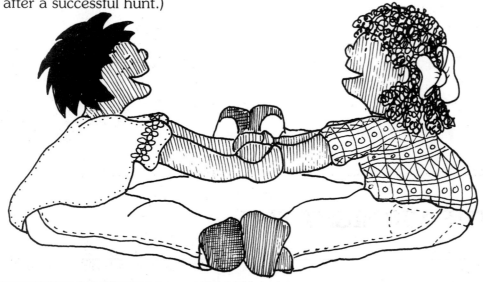

PARKA PARADE

Have the children wear their coats and hats for "parkas" and help them put on their mukluks and laced mittens from the Art activities on p. 151. Then play music and let them march around the room in a Parka Parade. If desired, let them use pan lids for "Eskimo hoop drums" and beat out the rhythm of the music with wooden spoons.

A-SLEDDING WE WILL GO

Sung to: "A-Hunting We Will Go"

A-sledding we will go,
Across the ice and snow.
Bow-wow the dogs will bark,
As over the ice we go.

We'll see some polar bears
Come out of their snowy lairs.
   (Move arms and shoulders up and down.)
Bow-wow the dogs will bark,
As over the ice we go.

We'll see some seals at play.
They'll slip and slide this way.
   (Move hands back and forth.)
Bow-wow the dogs will bark,
As over the ice we go.

Way out we'll see a whale.
   (Cup hand over eye.)
He'll wave at us with his tail.
   (Wave hand.)
Bow-wow the dogs will bark,
As over the ice we go.

We'll stop to fish and then,
   (Pretend to catch fish.)
We'll jump on the sled again.
   (Jump.)
Bow-wow the dogs will bark,
As over the ice we go.

Before singing the song, talk about how dog sleds are sometimes used for traveling over ice and snow in the Far North.

Elizabeth McKinnon

SALMON SNACKS

For a taste of Alaska, let the children sample pieces of canned salmon served on top of crackers. (Or substitute any other kinds of canned fish, if desired.) Accompany your snack with small cups of tea.

BEEF JERKY

Drying is a common way of preserving fish and game in Alaska. For your celebration serve beef jerky that is store-bought or made from the following recipe. Slice a 1- to 2-pound flank steak into $\frac{1}{4}$-inch strips and place them in a bowl. Make a marinade by combining $\frac{1}{4}$ cup soy sauce with $\frac{1}{4}$ cup Worcestershire sauce and adding onion salt, garlic powder, salt and pepper to taste. Cover the meat with the marinade and refrigerate for 6 to 8 hours, stirring occasionally. Drain the meat strips and place them on a rack over a shallow pan (or use a broiler pan). Then bake at 150 degrees for about 8 hours if you plan to serve the jerky right away. Otherwise, continue baking for 1 to 2 more hours, then cool and store in an airtight container.

ESKIMO ICE CREAM

A favorite treat often served at Eskimo gatherings is *agutuk* (Eskimo ice cream) made with sugar, fat and berries such as blueberries or salmon berries. For your celebration make "Eskimo ice cream" by mixing plain yogurt with unsweetened frozen apple juice concentrate to taste and stirring in blueberries. Add a few drops of vanilla, too, if desired. Then spoon the mixture into small cups and chill in the freezer until set.

WHY MR. FOX HAS A RED COAT

An Eskimo Folktale Adapted by Elizabeth McKinnon

Mrs. Mouse peeked out the door of her little underground burrow. It was very cold, and a few snowflakes were beginning to fall. "The ground will soon be covered with snow," she said. "I'd better go out and get some food for the winter."

Mrs. Mouse put on her fur parka, her fur mittens and her little fur boots. Then she took her little basket and hopped out of her burrow onto the frozen ground.

Not far from her door, Mrs. Mouse saw some tall grass bending and swaying in the wind. The seeds at the top were fat and ripe and just right for picking.

Mrs. Mouse scurried through the grass, gathering seeds to put in her basket. As she worked she kept a sharp eye out for Mr. Fox. In those days, Mr. Fox had a white coat. He could slip across the snow without being seen and catch any little mouse who wasn't being careful.

Soon Mrs. Mouse had filled her basket with seeds. "I'll take these inside and come back for more," she said.

But when Mrs. Mouse looked up, she saw something that made her little heart pound with fear. It was Mr. Fox staring at her through the grass with his big yellow eyes!

Mr. Fox smiled a wicked smile. Then he began to sing:

Mrs. Mouse is weak and small.
I'll gobble her up, ears, tail and all!

Mrs. Mouse was frightened, but she thought fast. "I know a song, too, Mr. Fox," she said. "But when I sing it, I have to hop."

Mrs. Mouse began hopping toward her door. And as she hopped she sang:

Mr. Fox has a snow-white coat.
He looks just like a nanny goat!

When Mr. Fox heard that, he was furious. He didn't like being compared to a nanny goat. He jumped at Mrs. Mouse, trying to catch her by the tail. But at that very moment, Mrs. Mouse reached her door. She hopped right through it and down into her little burrow.

"Oh, no!" cried Mr. Fox. "Mrs. Mouse tricked me! How could I have let such a tiny creature fool me like that?"

Mr. Fox was so embarrassed that he began to blush. First his face turned red. Then his back and his legs and his tail turned red too. Before long, he was red all over.

From that time on, Mr. Fox stayed away from Mrs. Mouse. But he never stopped being embarrassed about the trick she had played on him. That is why he never turned white again and why he still wears a red coat even to this day.

Totline newsletter.

Page for page, the *Totline* has more usable activities than any other early childhood education newsletter. Each bimonthly issue offers challenging and creative activities for children ages 2 to 6. Each issue of this indispensable resource includes suggestions for ◆ seasonal  themes ◆ learning games ◆ music and movement ◆ open-ended art ◆ language skills ◆ science activities ◆ children's book reviews ◆ and reproducible patterns and parent-flyer pages. **SAMPLE ISSUE: $2.**

Super Snack News.

This reproducible monthly newsletter is designed for parents. Each 4-page  issue is filled with ◆ nutritious snack recipes ◆ health tips ◆ and seasonal activities, including art, games, songs, and rhymes. Also included are portion guidelines for the CACFP government program. With each subscription you are given the right to make up to 200 copies. *Super Snack News* is great for parent involvement! **SAMPLE ISSUE: $1.**

Fresh ideas for parents and teachers of young children!

Keep up with what's new.

Keep up with what's appropriate.

Help your children feel good about themselves and their ability to learn.

Warren Publishing House, Inc.
P.O. Box 2250, Dept. Z
Everett, WA 98203

Hands-on, creative teaching ideas from Totline® books

PIGGYBACK® SONG SERIES

Piggyback Songs

More Piggyback Songs

Piggyback Songs for
  Infants and Toddlers

Piggyback Songs in
  Praise of God

Piggyback Songs in
  Praise of Jesus

Holiday Piggyback Songs

Animal Piggyback Songs

Piggyback Songs for School

Piggyback Songs to Sign

1•2•3 SERIES

1•2•3 Art

1•2•3 Games

1•2•3 Colors

1•2•3 Puppets

1•2•3 Murals

1•2•3 Books

1•2•3 Reading & Writing

1•2•3 Rhymes, Stories
  & Songs

1•2•3 Math

1•2•3 Science

MIX & MATCH PATTERNS

Animal Patterns

Everyday Patterns

Holiday Patterns

Nature Patterns

CUT & TELL SERIES

Scissor Stories for Fall

Scissor Stories for Winter

Scissor Stories for Spring

TEACHING TALE SERIES

Teeny-Tiny Folktales

Short-Short Stories

Mini-Mini Musicals

TAKE-HOME SERIES

Alphabet & Number Rhymes

Color, Shape & Season Rhymes

Object Rhymes

Animal Rhymes

THEME-A-SAURUS SERIES

Theme-A-Saurus

Theme-A-Saurus II

Toddler Theme-A-Saurus

Alphabet Theme-A-Saurus

Nursery Rhyme
  Theme-A-Saurus

Storytime Theme-A-Saurus

ABC SERIES

ABC Space

ABC Farm

ABC Zoo

ABC Circus

CELEBRATION SERIES

Small World Celebrations

Special Day Celebrations

Yankee Doodle
  Birthday Celebrations

Great Big Holiday Celebrations

LEARNING & CARING ABOUT

Our World

Our Selves

Our Town

1001 SERIES

1001 Teaching Props

1001 Teaching Tips

1001 Rhymes

EXPLORING SERIES

Exploring Sand

Exploring Water

Exploring Wood

OTHER

Super Snacks

Healthy Snacks

Teaching Snacks

Celebrating Childhood

Home Activity Booklet

23 Hands-On Workshops

Cooperation Booklet

Totline books are available at school-supply and parent-teacher stores.

 **Warren Publishing House, Inc.**